RSA
CORE TEXT
PROCESSING SKILLS

HEINEMANN
EDUCATIONAL
in association with the RSA Examinations Board

Heinemann Educational Books Ltd
Halley Court, Jordan Hill, Oxford OX2 8EJ

OXFORD LONDON EDINBURGH
MADRID ATHENS BOLOGNA PARIS
MELBOURNE SYDNEY AUCKLAND SINGAPORE TOKYO
IBADAN NAIROBI HARARE GABORONE
PORTSMOUTH NH (USA)

Company limited by guarantee in England: Registered 216181J.
Registered charity: number 327546. Registered office: Westwood Way, Coventry, CV4 8HS.

First published 1987

91 92 93 94 95 12 11 10 9 8 7 6 5 4 3

British Library Cataloguing in Publication Data

RSA core text processing skills
1. Word Processing
I. Royal Society of Arts
652'.5   Z52.4

ISBN 0-435-45182-0

Design and typesetting by The Pen and Ink Book Company Ltd, Huntingdon, Cambridgeshire

Printed in Great Britain by William Clowes Ltd, Beccles and London

Foreword

The RSA's schemes in Word Processing, Typewriting Skills, Audio-Transcription and Shorthand-Transcription are designed to develop the wide range of skills in which anyone working as a 'text processor' in today's office needs to attain competence. Consequently, the RSA's exams make extensive demands on the student's communication skills as well as on technical skills.

The new Core Text Processing Skills scheme has been developed in response to the need for a system of accrediting the skills that form the foundation for development of text processing competences. The scheme is closely related to the RSA's mainstream vocational text processing schemes but it must be made clear that the certificate is not intended to *represent an employable level of skill*: the criteria of speed, accuracy and presentation are there, of course, but the objectives are more limited and the standards students have to demonstrate in the exam are not designed to satisfy an employer. The underlying purpose of the scheme is to *develop general keyboarding/communication skills and attitudes that will both be useful to any pupil or individual in everyday life*, and will also ensure a flying start for those who later decide to go on to full vocational training in text processing and communication occupations.

Margaret Rees-Boughton, who prepared the first two very popular books in the RSA's series of publications, has prepared this text on the Core Text Processing Skills scheme in a way that offers the incentive of a stimulating pace and very immediate results to the student working through it. Once again, RSA's thanks are due to her for a realistic and innovative approach to the subject.

Martin Cross
Chief Executive
RSA Examinations Board

Contents

TASK 3

REPORT ON ACCIDENT

On Friday 24 (Septembre) the photocopiers in Room 126 were both in use
at 3 pm. Two operators and two people waiting for work to be completed
(was) in the room. as well as Two more people were also there including
one of ͜ injured persons, Miss Jamilla Prendhi.

When photocopying work has been completed it is placed on shelves
in the counter, facing the entrance door. The door is approached (into Room 126)
down two steps, and the door opens inwards.

Barry Johnson slipped on the two steps, which had just been washed.
He fell against the (door) and forced it open (quivkly). Jamilla, who (was)
was collecting papers from the counter shelves, was knocked over by the
door as Barry (fallen) into the room.

                                                    included
Details of injuries to both Jamilla and Barry will be ~~given~~ in Annex 1.

THE RSA EXAM: CORE TEXT PROCESSING SKILLS

The RSA exam in Core Text Processing Skills assesses:

- keyboarding;
- copying skill;
- using context to identify words;
- spelling;
- use of styles and conventions.

Present generations of pupils not equipped with these skills and abilities will be seriously disadvantaged in their personal and working lives.

The scheme is designed to be useful on a wide variety of courses, for both girls and boys. While much of the content is business-orientated, it is based on the sort of activities that individuals may engage in as part of everyday life.

While the application of knowledge and skills in this syllabus does not, at this level, constitute a vocational competence, it enhances communicative effectiveness in any discipline: catering students, those studying sciences, computer operators, nursing trainees, engineering and construction workers – all need the skills that enable them to use language and technology. More particularly, those who intend to go on to training specific to text processing occupations (word processing/typing, audio-typing, etc.) must demonstrate the aptitude accredited by this scheme.

MIXED ABILITIES

There will be a wide range of abilities and requirements among the people who wish to take the exam. Some will require only a familiarisation with a QWERTY keyboard, while others will want to develop fluent, eight-finger operation of the keyboard; some will have thorough knowledge of and skill in using English, while others will not yet have taken sufficient interest in what is required to be reliable in copying, spelling, correcting obvious errors of agreement or even spotting typographical mistakes.

In explaining and providing practice to meet the requirements of the RSA syllabus and exam in Core Text Processing Skills, this book sets out to provide a fast-moving learning programme, putting newly-acquired skills into use as soon as possible (e.g. typing a letter after eight keyboarding units).

Provision of too much material for repetitive practice encourages learners to believe that a set amount of work is essential for keyboard mastery at any level. As a result, learners who could make quicker progress often become bored, while those who ought to recognise their own weaknesses and to be put under pressure to make extra effort get no sense of urgency from plodding through what is presented as the 'norm'.

N.B. The front cover of every RSA Core Text Processing Skills exam paper contains some vital Notes for Candidates. These are always the same – see the first of these two Specimen Papers on page 89.

TASK 1

10 Fortune Cottages
Damson Common
LICHFIELD
Staffs B70 14TJ

Mrs J Roberts
26 Harman Way
Artwell Heath
DERBY DE8 9XQ

Type this personal letter on plain paper

Dear Mrs Roberts

I noticed your advert. in ~~the~~ this week's edition of The Journal and your offer to knit to order jumpers and skirts

My own bus. is based on machine-knitting and I often have a number of orders on hand at one time. ~~which~~ This makes it difficult to meet deadlines without help

It would be useful at such times to have help w. urgent orders. ~~However~~ It would be necy. for work to be produced ~~very~~ quickly, but I would not always be able to know in advance when urgent orders may be recd. If you agreed, I could ring you each Monday. I could then give you details of orders for that week.

If that seems suitable, please contact me by next Thurs.. We can then discuss further details.

Yrs. ffly.

TASK 2

Type an envelope for the above letter

By focusing on an essential core of practical information and activity this book encourages:

- a sense of achievement and progress for all, including the most able;
- discrimination among those objectives which an individual can master quickly, and those which demand further practice (i.e. identifying strengths and weaknesses);
- a sense of urgency in pupils with greater learning needs;
- maximum use of teaching skill through evaluation, with pupils, of particular weaknesses, and negotiation of the material and work needed for attainment of syllabus objectives;
- teachers to tailor extra work to the needs of individual student(s) to help overcome specific weaknesses in attaining objectives (rather than the most able being given extra general practice to mark time while average and weaker workers complete a repetitive programme).

The book provides:

- sufficient coverage of the keyboard for familiarisation in computer-based courses and for general use;
- some extra practice for those wishing to develop fluent eight-finger typing skill;
- specific guidance to candidates on each of the syllabus assessment objectives;
- exercises in spelling;
- practice in reading for meaning, including gaming, which aims to increase awareness of words and thereby improve copying and interpretation skills.

FIRST-TIME ACCURACY

The operator's keying speed is no longer the most significant factor in determining rate of production. Many machines can print at speeds unattainable manually, compensating for time taken to ensure that text is accurate before the command is given for it to be printed.

Therefore, this book gives relatively little emphasis to development of speed. First-time accuracy is stressed as most important in optimising the speed of modern office machinery.

Keying errors in use of computers cause unnecessary and often costly delays. Word processor operators who rely on repeated drafting become careless when keying, forgetting that the machine's facility for correction does not make finding errors easy, and that correcting many errors causes unnecessary delay.

In the exam, 300 words have to be typed, checked and corrected in one hour.

CORRECTIONS

The section on syllabus item C7 (see page 80) concentrates on results of correcting and how these will be assessed in the exam. There is no instruction on using specific machine correcting facilities. As considered appropriate for particular classes or groups, this must be taught or instructions obtained from a machine guide (manufacturer's or teacher's) to the equipment being used.

TASK 2

Type an envelope to go with the letter in Task 1

TASK 3

7
name
9

Re-type the Report. Make amendments shown, and correct the circled words

REPORT ON VISIT TO MIDLAND BANK PLC

operators
We were able to see ~~workers~~ working on a Sales Analysis program.
The details of our own requirements are almost the same as those
of the Bank, ~~and~~ so their program would seem to be suitable for
us. We have arranged for Mrs Jill Agers to visit our office.
She will give a demonstration using sample details from our
accounts.

took
Mr Jones-Sharpe then us to the Trustee Department. We met
Miss Jayne Fuller, who control their computer section. The
software being used did not equate with our needs for Trustee
there were
records, but other programs in the range which which would
meer our needs.
meet   opportunity.

We are grateful for the opprotunity to see the Midland Bank
operation. Please convey our thanks to Mr Sharpe and his
colleagues. We have arranged for the local agent for AD3LT III
to visit us next month.

Ref: 628/ATD/1987

USING MACHINE GUIDES

The ability to use machine guides is becoming an increasingly important activity in modern personal life as well as in office work. Whenever possible, this book instructs the learner to use a guide so as to develop this skill. It is hoped, therefore, that teachers will encourage pupils to follow written procedural instructions by restricting assistance to that which is necessary to help an individual achieve the purpose.

It may well be that pupils will need greatest help in the use of the guide index, particularly in identifying index headings likely to lead to the information required. They need encouragement to experiment and persevere until the right page is found; and to take note of the variety of data which may come to light on the way!

TOUCH TYPING

Reference has been made in this introduction to eight-finger typing, but learners are not exhorted to avoid looking at their machines and to keep their heads and eyes averted, concentrating on the draft they are copying. (This would make redundant, for example, the line-by-line correcting facility of electronic typewriters.)

It is suggested that pupils avoid looking at keys when actually typing, so as to build confidence in using all fingers, but that they are encouraged to look at their keyboards to find special characters as well as keys being used for the first time.

TASK 1

Type this personal letter on plain paper

23 Redmond Road

Firmount Park

LUTON

LU18 2BTB

Date.

Mrs A Goodwelle

Sales Director

Kenny's Kitchens Ltd

82-84 Abelson Road

LUTON

LU22 16XA

Dear Mrs Goodwelle

Thank you for your letter recd. today regarding about received. the damage to the wall cabinet recently fixed in my new kitchen. I am replying straight away because your letter refers to the colour as 'Rose'. Also, the sizes you state are not the same as my cabinet. whereas my units are 'Primrose' Perhaps you have confused me with someone else.

I sh. be glad if you will confirm that your representative should will def. call on Friday to repair the latch on my cabinet. definately If it is necy. to charge, I would like to know soon. I can necessary then go out on Fri. the day and make a sep. appointment for next separate week.

Yours sly. sincerely.

J Nicholls (Miss)

THE RSA EXAM:
CORE TEXT PROCESSING SKILLS

In this exam you can show you have basic skills and abilities which are:

a) an essential part of up-to-date communications in every occupation; and

b) the foundations of special training for jobs based on typewriting/ word processing, audio-typing, etc.

KEYBOARDING

First-time accuracy is the aim; speed is secondary. There are separate RSA Copy-Typing Speed Tests that you can enter to get a certificate showing your speed of keying.

COPYING

Copying involves:

- concentration;
- paying attention to detail;
- stamina;
- patience to check your work.

READING FOR MEANING

- **Handwriting/shorthand/audio** – all of these can contain the odd word(s) that you cannot read or hear easily. If you copy what you think the words say, you still need to read your typing to check that it makes sense. If it doesn't, it's wrong.
- **Amendments** – crossings-out and other alterations will be easy to follow if you read and understand the meaning of sentences.
- **Proof-reading** – checking work cannot be reliably and quickly done without understanding.

SPELLING

Executives (bosses) concentrate on the main message in letters, memos, etc. They rely on professional text processors to make sure that simple, everyday words are typed and spelt correctly.

COMMUNICATION CONVENTIONS

Executives also rely on text processors to set out material in a way that can be recognised as, for example, a letter, without giving instructions every time.

THE ROYAL SOCIETY OF ARTS
EXAMINATIONS BOARD

CORE TEXT PROCESSING SKILLS

SPECIMEN PAPER FOR 1986-87

(TIME ALLOWED - ONE HOUR)

Notes for Candidates

1 Please enter your name and centre number on each piece of your work.

2 Please assemble your completed work in the order in which it is presented in this paper and cross through any work which you do not wish to be marked.

3 Calculators and English dictionaries may be used in the examination.

————————————————

You must:

1 Complete all tasks.

2 Use only the stationery provided in your answer book.*

3 Insert today's date on the letter, unless otherwise instructed.

(Penalties will be incurred if these instructions are not followed.)

*Candidates using equipment which will not take the stationery provided may use stationery provided by the centre - a note must be made by the Invigilator on your answer book. If continuous stationery is used, the pages should be separated before insertion in your answer book.

STYLE

This refers to the presentation of items within documents, e.g. paragraphs, dates, abbreviations. Style of presentation is often a matter of personal, or company preference. Good style includes presenting the same type of item in the same way throughout a document.

MACHINE GUIDES

Typewriters

The manufacturers supply a booklet, or guide, showing the parts of your machine and examples of how to use them, usually including diagrams and/or photographs. You should take your time to study it, and to practise following the instructions.

Word processing equipment

Manufacturers' manuals are often difficult to follow. However, as well as the full manual, there is usually a smaller and easier-to-understand **guide**. This guide may be provided by the manufacturer or may have been prepared by your teacher.

If you are a beginner, the guide will be of greater assistance than the longer and more complicated manual(s).

Learning to use guides

You need to be able to use machine guides so that you can help yourself when working with new equipment. When complicated machines are introduced into an office, there is usually a training programme for the people who will use them; but it is difficult to remember everything that is packed into a short course. For some simpler machines there will be only a demonstration by the salesperson before you are left to use the new equipment.

If you train yourself to find information and to use instructions and diagrams to work out things for yourself, you will be increasing your working skills.

Here are three simple rules to help you:

Rule 1: always **go to the index**, but finding the right page numbers may not always be easy (see below).

Rule 2: always **keep looking** till you find what you want.

Rule 3: always **try out the instructions** (if necessary in different ways) **until they work**, and ask someone else's help rather than give up altogether.

The golden rule: **be patient**!

How to use your machine guide

To help you find the right page numbers in the indexes of typewriter and word processor guides (see rule 1 above), the machine parts listed on page 6 include possible headings which may lead you to the instructions you need.

Q When you are employed as a typist or word processor operator you will be processing work for others, who will be insulted if you think their work is of so little importance that it does not matter if it looks shoddy.

R Mary,who (no space)
no comma after 'job'
Company (should have small c)
Marys (apostrophe omitted)
sites; (should be colon ':')
Chingford.Mary (no space after full stop)
Chingford, (should be full stop '.')
" Why (space after quotation marks)
Chingford?"Mary (no space after closing quotation marks)
reply: (should be semi-colon ';')
reason (reasons)

Total: 11 word faults

S

¹A	D	²V	E	R	³T	⁴I	⁵S	E	M	⁶E	N	⁷T
C		E			⁸W	E	T			N		A
⁹C	U	R	E				¹⁰O	¹¹L	¹²I	V	E	S
O		B				¹³S	P	A	C	E		T
¹⁴M	U	S	¹⁵T				¹⁶T	E	L	L	Y
M		O			¹⁷D		E		O		
O			¹⁸F	A	N				²⁰P	²¹A	²²T
²³D	E	²⁴F	I	N	I	T	E		²⁵M	E	M	O
A		U		²⁶T	E	X	²⁷T				
²⁸T	O	L	²⁹D			³⁰T	R	A	I	N	³¹S
I		³²L	I	F	T	³³S		U			I
³⁴O	H		R			P		L		³⁵O	³⁶U	R
³⁷N	E	C	E	S	S	A	R	Y		³⁸P	S

T We thank *you* for *your* letter and can inform you that *the* goods on your order will be despatched by *30* June. Please confirm the *address* of your works is still:

Fairfax Industrial Site LIVERPOOL L21 4DO.

With reference *to* your account, our Sales Ledger Department has received your comments and will *contact* you in the next few *days*.

1 Typewriters

Use the machine guide to find out how to:	Possible index headings
a) put paper into the machine	paper feed inserting paper paper insertion
b) straighten your paper	paper release paper guide paper scale paper bail
c) set a left margin	margin stop margin keys
d) move to a new line	return carriage return lever
e) change letters (to correct any errors you make in keying)*	LED, correcting, editing (electronic machines) lift-off tape, correcting ribbon

*If you are using a manual typewriter you need to have correcting fluid (with thinners), or correction paper (or plastic) slips or a typewriter eraser (rubber).

2 Word processing equipment

You need to know how to:	Possible index headings
a) start up your system	getting started switching-on
b) switch to text screen	opening a file new files text screen keying-in or entering text
c) follow your typing position on the screen, using the cursor	cursor editing
d) move to next line; leave lines clear, i.e. without typing	return wrap-around
e) change letters on screen (to correct any errors you make in keying)	editing deleting, inserting
f) print work with margins no less than 13 mm (half-inch)	save and print print margins page format
g) use A4 paper and DL envelopes (see also pages 24, 55 and 68)	printing

N

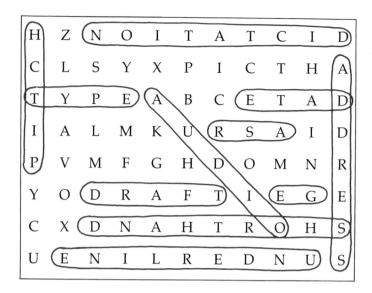

O

DECISION-MAKING IMPROVES YOUR TEXT PROCESSING
PRODUCTION RATE

Production work is equal in importance to the learning of the keyboard and building speed and accuracy. However, students often learn to type and are then expected to produce work without training in making decisions for production typing and production word processing.

Production not only involves skills in keyboarding but also requires skills in making machine adjustments, handling materials, reading directions, planning the total job, proofreading, correcting errors and disposing of the completed papers. Most of the time-consuming elements of production have nothing to do with speed of keyboarding.

P

```
B   X   W   Y   P   Q   T   N
↓                           ↓
U   F   D   R   C   E   W   P
↓                           ↓
Y ► Y ► O ► U ► R ► O   X   A
                            ↓
B ◄ N ◄ O ◄ O ◄ S   Z   Q   P
↓                           ↓
E   I ► D ► E   L   W   O   E
↓   ▲       ▲               ↓
U   S   I ◄ S   L   R   M   R
↓   ▲   ↓   ▲               ↓
S   H   T ► I   I   X   Q   A
↓   ▲   ↓   ▲               ↓
I   T   T ◄ S   W   P   Z   N
↓   ▲   ↓   ▲               ↓
N   O   O   I   U ◄ O ◄ Y ◄ D
↓   ▲   ↓
G ► B   O ► D ► E ► A ► R ► T
                            ↓
X   W   E ◄ T ◄ S ◄ A ◄ W ◄ O
```

Buy your own paper and you will soon be using both sides. It is too dear to waste.

1 AIMS

This scheme defines those skills which are the foundations of processing original and edited text using either a typewriter or word processing equipment. Competence in these basic skills is measured as a totality of speed, accuracy and presentation of work. Candidates will be assessed in each of these 3 elements and for award of a certificate must meet the criteria specified for all 3 of them (see paragraphs 6.2 and 6.3).

The overall aim is to accredit skills as a basis for progression to text processing competences at RSA Stage I level (Typewriting, Word Processing, Audio-Transcription).

2 TARGET POPULATION

The beginner typist or word processor operator who has sufficient machine knowledge, command of English and the conventions of written communication to process simple legible drafts.

3 ASSESSMENT OBJECTIVES

Section A – Rate of production

A   Candidates must use their machines to work at a rate of production* adequate to complete 3 tasks within 1 hour.

Working from handwritten and typewritten drafts within the 3 tasks they must produce:

A1   Personal letter
A2   Envelope†
A3   Business document in continuous text

*The production rate at this level takes into account time for: machine manipulation, organisation of time and materials, scanning, reading, interpreting (including use of context to identify words as necessary), use of styles and conventions, checking and correcting, for the purpose of processing drafts in any context.

†Candidates using word processing equipment may use a typewriter to produce the envelope. Alternatively, centres, at their own discretion, may provide labels for use with their word processing equipment which should then be adhered to the envelope provided.

Section B – Accuracy of content

B   Candidates must use their machines to produce work which, after application of appropriate correction techniques/materials, is accurate in content.

They must:

B1   INSERT date on letters

B2   INCORPORATE amendments to text:

a) deletions with replacement
b) deletions without replacement
c) correction sign for insertions: ⋏ with words above; balloon with arrow

B3   SPELL the following words accurately from the abbreviations as shown:

accom.	accommodation
advert(s).	advertisement(s)
bel.	believe
bus.	business
co(s).	company/ies
def.	definite/ly

H

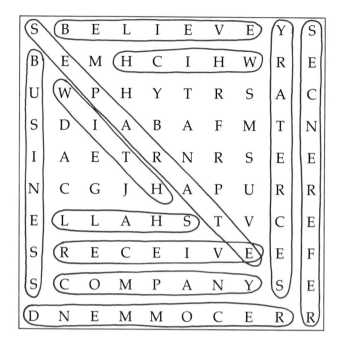

I Differences occur in lines 1, 2, 5, 6, 7, 8, 9, 10, 11, 12, 14 and 15.

J The following words are incorrect in the typed example:

road; unddertaken; holiday; 'not' omitted; an extra word 'ride' included; 'fishponds' should be two words; by; 'with protective netting' omitted; hyphen omitted from 'weed-killers'; an extra 'be' included; 'an' omitted; unlabeled; containers.

K Differences occur in lines 7, 10, 11, 13, 14, 15, 19, 20, 21, 23, 25, 26 and 28.

L We are now able to advise you that your order for Garden Tools is ready for despatch. However, we understand following your telephone call yesterday that you may prefer to collect these items. We were unable to contact you by phone today. The goods will be available for collection on Monday next, any time after 9 am. However, if you do wish us to send them, please let us know as soon as possible.

M 1 by, unable, look

2 heard, acting, effect, their, definitely, Robinson, willing, made, is

3 comprises, loose, guttering, work repaired, No

4 supposed, lovers, families, take, addition, thought

necy.	necessary
opp(s).	opportunity/ies
rec.	receive
recd.	received
recom.	recommend
ref(s).	reference(s)
resp.	responsible
sec(s).	secretary/ies
sep.	separate
thro'	through
sh.	shall
wh.	which
w.	with

days of the week (e.g. Thurs., Fri.)
months of the year (e.g. Jan., Feb.)
words in addresses (e.g. Cres., Dr.)
complimentary closes (e.g. ffly.)

(N.B. full stops with the words above indicate abbreviations, not punctuation)

B4   ADDRESS envelopes as instructed*

B5   COPY unfamiliar and/or foreign words from legible draft

B6   PRESENT IN CORRECTED FORM material containing:

a) obvious typographical errors
b) obvious errors of agreement

These errors will be circled in the draft, and will be confined to one specified task in typescript.

*See note under A2

Section C – Presentation of work

C   Candidates must use their machines to produce work which, after application of appropriate correction techniques/materials, is effectively presented and in line with general conventions.

They must:

C1   IDENTIFY and USE A4 sheets and DL manilla envelopes without undue waste

N.B.   i) Candidates using equipment which will not take the stationery provided may use stationery provided by the centre; a note should be made by the Invigilator on the candidate's answer folder. If continuous stationery is used, the pages should be separated before insertion in the candidate's folder.
ii) See note under A2 concerning envelopes.

C2   PRODUCE clean, uncreased work

N.B. Candidates using word processors must ensure that the printout of their tasks is clean and uncreased, if necessary requesting a further printout.

C3   ENSURE CONSISTENCY throughout a task in the style or form of presentation (at own discretion in the absence of instructions) of the following:

a) *Punctuation*: Consistent number of spaces after punctuation marks;

Consistent use of open punctuation (that is omission of ornamental commas and full stops)
or consistent use of full punctuation (that is insertion of both grammatical and ornamental commas and full stops).

A   secretary secretaries secretarial secretariat

advertise advertiser advertises advertised advertising advertisement/s

define defines defined definer definition/s definite/ly

receive receives received receiver receiving receipt receipts receipted

refer refers referred reference references referenced

B   We [*subject*] shall be [*action – verb*] glad of your co-operation in this matter [*description of* **what** *we shall be*].

By next Thursday [*description*] we [*subject*] shall have [*verb – what we shall do*] the goods [*more description*].

With reference to your letter of yesterday [*description*], we [*subject*] have passed [*verb – says what action we have taken*] your request to our Accounts Department [*more description*].

C   A noun is a *word* used as a *name* for a thing, place or person. Names of particular *people* or *places* must be given a capital letter. Names of businesses, associations, societies and clubs must also have *capital letters* and you should always use a capital letter for the word 'I'.

D   With reference to your letter dated 10 January I believe you will be able to move into your new home next month. Mr Jones has already paid a deposit on the house in Poole and expects to move no later than 15 March. Contracts cannot be exchanged until Building Society approval is given.

E   The book shelves were very untidy with about fifty books on each shelf. Sandra and Jason were asked to tidy them and to sort the books into alphabetical order. Sandra thought they should use the names of the authors to do this but Jason wanted to sort the titles into alphabetical order. After arguing for several minutes they went to the office to ask Alphonse to explain. He was speaking on the telephone and they had to wait a few more minutes. By then it was nearly lunchtime so after Alphonse had explained that the authors should be in alphabetical order and that he would help, they all agreed to start the sorting in the afternoon.

F   With regard to your request for a discount our Branch Manager informs me that the prices quoted already include a reduction of 10%. I hope you will agree this makes the cost of the Garden Tools very competitive. Invoice No 627 is enclosed for goods supplied in August and we hope to receive your cheque soon.

G   Examples of words you may have found:

Three-letter words: fen gun den bud cut cur rut rug mud jet red yet
Four-letter words: dumb nude hunt mend butt herd true tend dent rung turn vent vend bend fend Bury June Ruth Fred Greg grey free jury term fern tern
Five-letter words: crumb there truth grunt brute demur dummy muddy teeth Brent Rugby Derby jetty jemmy deuce Gerry green deter fence greed mummy never
Six-letter words: denude defend crunch demure tether cruder church judged dredge numbed number member duffer refund thence
Seven- (or more) letter words: thunder thundered dredger dredged numbered refunded grunted

(Invigilators must report any cases of candidates using machines on which justified margin is permanently used.)

b) *Line spacing*: i.e. all paragraphs in same (single- or double-) line spacing and consistent number of clear lines between paragraphs.

C4 USE capitals and underlining (for emphasis in headings and in text) as shown in draft

C5 Typewriting candidates:

USE regular left-hand and top margins of at least ½ inch

Word Processing candidates:

ENSURE an aggregate right and left margin of at least one inch

C6 LEAVE a *minimum* of one clear line space

a) before and after headings
b) between complimentary close and signatory
c) before and after separate items within a document e.g. date, inside address.

C7 USE CORRECTING MATERIALS/TECHNIQUES as necessary to make inconspicuous corrections

4   FORM OF ASSESSMENT

4.1 Candidates will be assessed in a 1-hour production test set and marked by the RSA and consisting of 3 practical tasks presented in handwriting and typescript.

4.2 Nature of tasks: the material given will be general and personal documentation in work-related contexts, e.g. letters of complaint, enquiries, job applications, extracts from reports.

4.3 The stationery provided for completion of tasks will be:

A4 plain white   6
DL manilla envelopes   2

No additional stationery will be allowed. *Also* see note under C1

4.4 Candidates may use calculators, English and mother-tongue dictionaries, on-line spellcheckers and centre-prepared or manufacturers' manuals in the examination. The RSA does not provide these, or correcting materials, and candidates are advised to check with their centres well before the examination whether they need to bring any of them.

4.5 Any form of correcting material/mechanism may be used.

4.6 On equipment where printing is not simultaneous with the keying operation, hard copy may be produced outside the one hour allowed but no amendments can be made to the text after that time has expired. The printing may be carried out by the tutor or any other person appointed by the Local Secretary.

5   CRITERIA OF ASSESSMENT

Marking Scheme

Obvious machine faults will not be penalised

A   *Production rate* – all tasks to be completed (except for omissions at the end of tasks, which may be counted within tolerances for Section B, see paragraph 6).

Type

Type this letter, with an envelope

124 Chambers Ave.
Durham Villas
BLACKBURN BB41 8TB

Dear Mrs Kidger

Thank you for your letter. The accom. occupied by your son, Barry, has now been let and a cheque for £15 is being sent to you tomorrow by the Agent.

I have looked thro' the clothes left by Barry to be given to Mary next month, and have found a key. I may be it the one he is looking for, and it will be sent with the cheque tomorrow.

Best wishes to you & all of your family.

Yrs. sdy.

Mrs E Kidger
67 Landley St.
SLOUGH SL26 4DJ

Within 20 minutes your work should be absolutely accurate. This task is more difficult than the ones that you will be given in the RSA Core Text Processing Skills exam, so you will be well prepared for the exam when you can do work as hard as this task.

B   *Accuracy of content*

An Accuracy fault is ascribed to any word not 100% accurate when compared with the draft.

A word is defined as:

a) any normally recognisable word (hyphenated words count as one).
b) any series of characters (including spaces where appropriate) which constitute a recognisable unit, e.g. postcode, initials or groups of initials, courtesy title, line of dots, line of ruling, numbers, simple or compound measurements.
c) including following or associated punctuation and spacing.

One Accuracy fault only will be ascribed to any one word (e.g. 'acommodatoin' counts only as one Accuracy fault in spite of several faults in the word) but Presentation faults may be applied in addition.

The same fault appearing more than once counts as an Accuracy fault each time.

Envelopes will be treated in the same way as all other pieces of work and will be marked in the usual way.

There are three main types of Accuracy fault:

1   *Typing/keying/spelling/punctuation faults*:

These are words which:

1.1   contain a character which is incorrect or illegible for any reason

1.2   have omitted or additional characters or spaces within the word (including omissions caused by faulty use of correction materials/ techniques, e.g. hole in paper)

1.3   contain handwritten characters

1.4   have no space following them; have more than 2 spaces following them, except where necessary or appropriate e.g. before postcodes or in work with justified margins

1.5   contain overtyping
      (Satisfactory stretching or squeezing of words without overlapping will not be penalised.)

1.6   do not contain initial capitals which are shown in draft, or contain initial capitals which are not shown in draft.

2   *Omissions and additions*:

One Accuracy fault will be ascribed to:

2.1   each word which is:

      – the wrong word (replacing a word)
      – omitted (and not replaced)
      – added (not replacing a word)
2.2   each instance of failure to indicate paragraph as per draft.

3   *Transpositions and misplacements*:

One Accuracy fault will be ascribed to each instance of words:

      – inserted in wrong order or place, e.g. misplaced within text or as foot or marginal note, regardless of the amount of material involved (in addition to any Accuracy faults which may be incurred under B.1 above).

Read   In this book time allowed for 'typing' includes time for:

- preparation before starting to key-in;
- keying;
- checking and correcting your work;
- printing time for word processing equipment.

Many people find it difficult to prepare before starting to type, because they find it boring. This may be because they do not have a routine to follow.

Outlined below is a suggested preparation routine:

- Find each word which has been shortened in the draft:
  – decide if the word should be typed in full;
  – if so, write down the full spelling (e.g. on a notepad or, in the exam, on the question paper), checking in your dictionary if necessary.

- Find each handwritten amendment in the draft:
  – read through the alteration;
  – read the whole sentence to make sure that you have read the alteration correctly.

- Check what type of document the draft is intended to be:
  – if it is a letter, add a note to the draft to include the date.

- Find each instruction:
  – read what it tells you to do;
  – find, in the draft, the place(s) where you must remember the instruction(s);
  – make pencil marks on the draft to remind you (you should erase them later if the draft is in a book that someone else is going to use after you);
  – make any machine adjustments necessary, e.g. for line spacing.

- **Read** the document to make sure you can read all of the words, to understand its meaning and to check punctuation.

This seems a long list, but if you get yourself into the habit of following the routine it will become automatic – you'll do it quickly, and you'll save yourself time in the long run, as well as avoiding unnecessary mistakes (and exam penalties!).

C *Presentation of work*

One presentation fault will be recorded for each:

C1 task on incorrect stationery

C2 task dirty (e.g. with thumb marks, eraser stains, typing on reverse), creased or torn

C3 inconsistency in the following:

a) punctuation – spacing after (unless right justification is impossible to turn off)(at least one space required after punctuation mark)
(N.B. if *no* space, Accuracy fault – see B1.4)
open/full

b) line spacing – paragraphs in single/double between paragraphs

C4 instance of capitals/underlinings in headings and in text not as shown in draft

(Unrequested underlining or emboldening of headings will not be penalised. Consistent incorrect use of capitals/underlining in related headings within a task = 1 fault only)

C5 Typewriting candidates:

Top margin less than 13 mm (½") ⎤ either or
Left margin less than 13 mm (½") ⎦ both margins

Word Processing candidates:

aggregate left and right margin of less than 25 mm (1")

Task with irregular left margin not attributable to machine fault nor to intentional variance for sub-paragraphs, listed items, etc.

C6 instance of NO clear line space, in the absence of instructions, at points a) to c) – ONE penalty only throughout a task for each item:

a) before and after headings
b) between complimentary close and signatory
c) before and after separate items within a document

C7 instance (may be one or more words) of unsightly and conspicuous correction that results in:

a) characters appearing blurred or bold in contrast with uncorrected work
b) smoothness of paper being impaired by raised peaks of correcting fluid (N.B. no penalty for unavoidable raised effect of use of fluid or stick-on tapes/strips)
c) substantial misalignment of character(s) – i.e. half-line space or more (N.B. no penalty for direct typing on copies for correction purposes)
d) hole in paper – unless already penalised under B1.2 as an Accuracy fault

(White correcting fluid on coloured stationery will not be penalised.)

Type the following, reading for meaning as you type so that you can spot and correct the deliberate error(s):

Type

> We thank you you for you letter and can inform you that the
> the goods on your order will be despatched by 30 June. Pease
> confirm the adrdess of your works is still:
>
> Fairfax Industrial Site LIVERPOOL L21 4DO.
>
> With reference t1 your account, our Sales Ledger Department
> has received your comments and will cotnact you in the next
> few day.s

Check yourself

Check your work with the key on page 88, **T**.

6 CERTIFICATION

6.1 Results will be graded Distinction, Pass or Fail.

6.2 For award of a Certificate with Distinction candidates must fulfil
Objective A by working at a production rate of 300 words per hour (i.e. completing all the 3 tasks);
Objective B with no more than 15 Accuracy faults;

and

Objective C with no more than 9 Presentation faults.

6.3 For award of a Pass Certificate candidates must fulfil
Objective A by working at a production rate of 300 words per hour
(i.e. completing all the 3 tasks);
Objective B with no more than 45 Accuracy faults;

and

Objective C with no more than 15 Presentation faults.

6.4 The results slip issued to all candidates will indicate the grade awarded on each of the three elements of the assessment; and whether the work was done on a typewriter or word processing equipment.

If you sometimes have to use a machine which does not have a correcting ribbon or lift-off tape you need to remember to change your method, or you could be overtyping and be penalised for accuracy faults.

Type the following exactly, then correct the deliberate error(s) without retyping the whole:

Type

```
This repot  is based on information given in March 1987 and

recommendations which were made in The Journal. The stati-

istics will also by includes in The Company Review next year.
```

Read

Correcting fluid

Correcting fluid is bound to be visible in most cases, but you will not be penalised for sensible use of fluid in correcting work:

1   let fluid dry before typing over it:
   - if the correct letters (or figures) are blurred in your work you will be penalised with a **presentation fault**.
   - you will also receive a penalty for presentation if the corrected letters/figures stand out (bold) in heavy type because of poor correction.
2   do not use thick or lumpy fluid – use thinners to keep it runny:
   - presentation faults will be incurred if the fluid causes roughness on the paper.

Correcting papers/plastic sheets

It is also important to use correcting papers/plastic sheets carefully:

- make sure the correcting material is not already used up at the point you are going to use for your correction. If it is, you may have to do it again, and need to 'thump' the keys to make the correct letter show. You could then be penalised for a presentation fault because of blurred or bold corrections.

Typewriter erasers

Using these takes patience, because if you rub hard and quickly you can make the paper rough – or even tear a hole:

- if the paper is rubbed rough, new characters typed will appear blurred or bold, and your work will be penalised for presentation
- if there is a hole where there should be a letter in a word, you will be penalised for inaccuracy because the word has letter(s) missing; if you make a hole in the paper where there is no word, for example, in the margin, your work will be penalised for a presentation fault.

LETTERS r, t, f, g, v, b AND SPACE BAR

FIRST *finger* LEFT *hand*

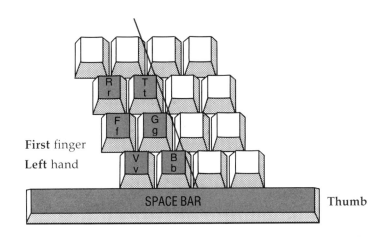

First finger
Left hand

SPACE BAR   Thumb

Type	r t f g v b (return)

Tap the space bar to leave a space between each letter

You need to get the *feel* of these letters in your finger.

Type	f r f t f g f v f b f (return)

You can't use this finger on its own to type **words** because there are no **vowels** to link the letters to make word sounds.

Type	f r t f g f v b f (return)
	f t f r f g f v f b f t f (return)

Check yourself	*Aim to type the following accurately without stopping:*
	r t f g v b (return)
	f t f r f g f v f b f t f (return)
	t f r f g f v f b (return)

Read	Practise **checking** your work. This does not mean just 'reading' it. What you have typed may make sense, but if you read only your typing you may not notice differences between it and what you should have copied (the draft).

Check your typing of the three lines above – follow letters *and* spaces in the book with your finger, and follow your typing with your other hand.

If you have made mistakes, retype the three lines.

C7 CORRECTING YOUR OWN WORK

Read

In the exam you will be penalised if you do not find and correct your own mistakes.

Each word which has uncorrected error(s) will be counted as an accuracy fault.

Each word with a letter missing will be counted as an accuracy fault – even though you may have started to correct it and, say, forgotten to type in the correct letter(s). This could also happen if you were using a typewriter eraser and rubbed a hole in the paper!

Each word with an overtype will be counted as an accuracy fault. This may happen with typewriters if you do not attempt to correct properly but just type over the error; or you may try to correct it but leave too much of the error uncovered or unerased when you type in the new letter(s). This, of course, cannot happen with word processing equipment.

Correcting errors using word processors

Word processing equipment corrects errors without trace – but only if you know and use the techniques properly. Use the guide to your particular machine to find the best way of using the editing facilities to correct errors. But remember, you still have to watch and read your screen carefully so as to find your errors – and correcting still takes time.

Electronic typewriters with one-line display

With these machines you need to watch for errors in the display 'window' so as to correct them before the line is printed. Your machine guide will show you how to correct miskeyed words, usually by use of the backspace key and typing the new, correct letter(s) over the error(s).

If you sometimes use other machines that do not have one-line display and correction, remember that any overtyping in your work will result in penalty. You have to change your method to suit different machines.

*Type the following **exactly**, then correct the deliberate error(s):*

Type

```
I cannit attenx the mettting on the 16 Octobdr because I am

due to be in london at 11 o'clock.
```

Read

Lift-off or correcting tape

When using a typewriter with lift-off or correcting tape you will also be able to make corrections that will be regarded as inconspicuous (that is, they do not catch the eye immediately on looking at the page). Your machine guide will give clear instructions on how to use the tape to make corrections.

You should remember that correcting tapes are expensive, and you should not use them carelessly or you will not be popular with whoever pays for them.

LETTERS y, u, h, j, n, m

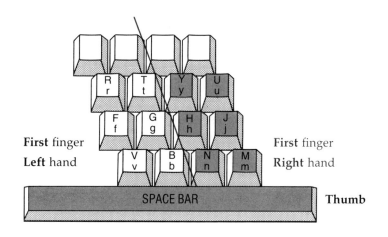

FIRST finger RIGHT hand

Type   j u j m j y j h j n j m j (return)

Type the above line again, following the pattern of your finger movements. You'll soon realise that your finger always comes back to rest on the 'j'. If you rest your fingers on the middle row of letter keys you can find and reach the other keys more easily.

Type   j h j n j m j h j y j u m j (return)

Now you can type **words** because you have the 'u', which is a vowel, and the 'y', which can be used as a vowel, to link letters into word sounds.

BOTH HANDS: look at the chart above to see where the letters are (and try to avoid looking at the keys when typing).

Type

jug mug hug (return)   buy guy try   (return)

run nun bun (return)   turf turn burn   (return)

but tub nut (return)   hymn trug grub   (return)

Check yourself

Aim to type the following accurately without stopping:

jug run but buy turf trug   (return)

Remember, every letter and each space must be exactly as the example above before you can claim to have typed **accurately**–so don't be surprised if you need several tries before you succeed.

Read

You may prefer to leave more than one clear line to separate headings, particularly main headings at the top of the page, from the text below them. For example, in the exercise on page 78 you may have wished to leave two clear lines before 'AGENDA' and before 'Documents' as well as after the main heading 'NOTICE OF MEETING'.

In the exam you will not be penalised for leaving more than one clear line before and after headings, so long as you leave at least one, and the **same** number of clear lines before and after the same type of heading throughout a task.

Space between complimentary close (e.g. Yours faithfully) and signatory (person signing)

In the practice letters in this book you have been reminded to leave several lines for the person sending the letter to sign it.

There is no special rule about how many spaces to leave because signatures differ so much in size. It is something that you would have to check each time you type work for a different person.

A general rule you could adopt is to leave four clear lines, but **in the exam** you will not be penalised unless you forget to leave any space at all for the signature.

Practise leaving room for a signature in documents other than letters.

Re-type the following, correcting the words circled and amending as required:

Type

REPORT ON CATALOGUE PRODUCTION

I am glad to report that the preparation of the autumn catalogues (are) now proceeding well. The final proofs of the ASPECTS catalogue, the SCENE TWO catalogue and the Accessories list will be (available) last Wednesday. *next* I shall be glad if you can confirm you will be available to check these on Thursday, Friday and Monday so that they ~~have~~ *can be* returned with corrections on Tuesday (to Print Section).

If, *as usual,* you intend to send out the *new* spring ~~1988~~ catalogues early in the new year please let me have the material by the first week in September so that preparations can be put in hand in good time.

JMT (leave room for us to initial. JMT)

(Today's date) ◄————————————————

You must remember always to date letters without having to be reminded every time. But if other documents (such as this one) are to be dated, special instructions will be given.

Check yourself

1 Did you type the circled words as follows: is (related to 'preparation'), available?
2 Did you:

a) type today's date accurately?
b) leave room for the initials, at least large enough for the initials as signed in the instruction?
c) leave at least one line clear after the heading and between the paragraphs?
3 It is not an error if you typed the report in double-line spacing – but if so, did you leave extra space to show where the new paragraph starts?

THE SHIFT KEY

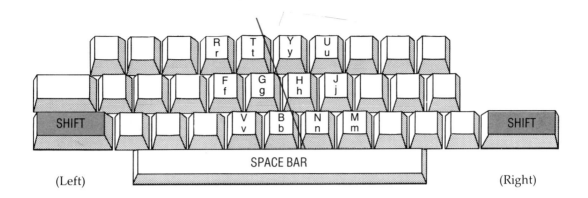

(Left)   (Right)

Hold down the **LEFT** shift key (use your little finger) while you type a letter with your **right** hand:

Type

Mr Hugh Jutt

Mr J H Yungh

Check yourself

If your capital letters appear higher than the small letters (i.e. above, not on, the line), you did not hold down the shift key for long enough; but you must remember to take your finger off the shift key once you have typed a capital so that you can go back to the small letters.

Use your **RIGHT-HAND** little finger to hold down the other shift key while you type a letter with your **left** hand:

Type

Burt Trygh

Guy Vynth

TWO HANDS: look at the chart at the top of the page to find the letters, and to work out which shift key to use:

Type

Mr Grumb

Mr Hugh Gruvy

Mr J Vynt

Mr V Bunty

Check yourself

Aim to type the following accurately without stopping. Use 'return' at the end of each line. **Proper** nouns must be typed with a capital letter because they are the names of people or places.

Mr Gumm fry try Mr Hugh Gruvy
Mr J Vynt tub fun Mr H Grumb
Mr V Bunty numb rub hub

C6 SEPARATING DIFFERENT PARTS OF A DOCUMENT

Read Throughout the practice material and the checking sections in this book you have been reminded that the different items within any document need to be separated by at least one clear line space, that is, a line without any typing. This makes the document easier to read, and the separate items easier to find if you have to refer to them later.

Space between paragraphs

On page 73 there are illustrations and 'rules' for spacing between paragraphs.

Space before and after headings

Practise leaving space so as to separate headings from text:

Type

NOTICE OF MEETING

Meeting No 6/27/88 ~~will~~ of the Technical Aid Committee will be held on Wed. 6 Jan. 1988 at 1430 hrs in Room T103 at JOHN ADAM ST. LONDON WC2 6EZ.

AGENDA

1 To rec. apologies for absence.
2 To confirm minutes of the l~~f~~ast meeting.
3 To ~~discuss~~ *note* correspondence recd..
4 To determine details of expenditure for the final quarter of the financial year.
5 To decide date of next meeting.
6 Any Other Business.

Documents
5/27/87   Minutes
88/001   Financial Accounts
88/002   Departmental Budgets

> Leave the SAME NUMBER of spaces here to separate figures from items

Check yourself

1 Did you spell the following words correctly: Wednesday, January, Street, receive, received?
2 Did you:
   a) leave at least one clear line above and below headings and between paragraphs, including the numbered lines?
   b) use capitals and underlining exactly as shown in the draft?

THE SHIFT LOCK, UNDERLINE AND BACKSPACE KEYS

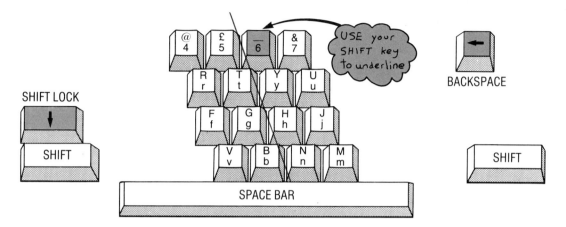

Look at your keyboard to find:

1 the **shift lock**;
2 the **underline key** (it is a right-hand **first finger** key on the illustrated keyboard above)
3 the **backspace key** (see the keyboard above).

Read   Underlining emphasises (shows the importance of) words or headings. If you are using word processing equipment, see page 17.

Typewriters

After typing a word to be underlined, **backspace** to its beginning; put on the **shift lock**; **underline** the exact number of letters in the word (it is not good practice for underlining to 'hang over' at one end, e.g. Stations̲ . Remember to release the shift lock before typing the next word.

Type

<u>Hugh</u> bun fry my

Try <u>my</u> mug

Mr Guy <u>Tunn</u>

Check yourself   *Type the following.* Underline every word with double-letters (e.g. <u>butt</u>y):

butty nutty hurt tummy numb

judge grubby gun buggy fury

bunny thumb funny fry thy

Decide what margins to use at the top and left edge of your paper for the following letter. *Type the letter and an envelope:*

Type

26 Fortune Way
Derry Park
MANCHESTER M17 4DR

Messrs James & Oscarlen
Parity House
Derby Ave.
MANCHESTER M21 6XX

Dear Sirs

W. ref. to your advert. for a junior clerk, I sh. be glad if you will consider my application for the post.

I enclose my CV together w. two refs.. You will see I have six months' experience in the office of a co. similar to yours as part of a YTS course. I therefore feel I can cope very well w. the type of work outlined in your advert. and could adapt to other reap$onsibilities in due course.

As I am presently unemployed I can attend for interview at any time. However, if you required me to attend on Tues. or Thurs. morning I would be glad of at least one full day's notice so that I could excuse mysey from the class I attend then in Word Processing.

This is a reminder that there are items to be ENCLOSED when the letter is posted. Just copy this where it appears. You know you must leave room for the letter to be signed, so first leave clear line spaces for a signature. Then turn up at least another two single-line spaces to separate 'Encs' from the signature.

Yrs. ffly.

Encs.

(I look forward to receiving a favourable reply.)

Check yourself

1 Did you type the following in full: Avenue, with, reference, advertisement, shall, references, company, Tuesday, Thursday, Yours faithfully?

2 Did you:

   a) remember to date the letter?
   b) leave a clear line to separate the different items in the letter?
   c) leave several lines for a signature before copying 'Enc' at the margin?
   d) type an envelope?

3 Does the letter 'fit' the paper well, or would you change the margins if you were asked to type the letter again?

Word processing equipment

Use your
machine
manual

Look up 'underline' and practise by following the instructions in your manual until you are confident that you know how to underline.

Find out

It may not be possible to **underline** when using your word processing equipment. If this is so, you should **find out** how to use the **emboldening** function to **highlight** words. A **highlighting** function may include the ability to underline *or* to type in bold letters.

If the word processor that you are using can underline, copy the exercises on page 16 with the words underlined.

If you are not able to underline, use the highlighting, bold, or embolden function on your machine instead to present the underlined words on page 16.

You should also follow this procedure in the RSA exam in Core Text Processing Skills (see page 75).

Type the following letter, spelling all of the shortened words in full, making all of the amendments shown, and copying capitals:

Type

Basingstoke Hse.
Charlestone Rd.
BIRMINGHAM B90 4DY

Dear Mr Davidson

I am in receipt of your letter ~~dictated to~~ w. ref. to your application for
tickets ~~the the~~ to our annual show. My sec., John Downes, is resp. for the
allocation of seats, and if you will telephone him on 021-996 1234, extension 57,
w. full details of your requirements, he will arrange to forward tickets to you.

yrs. truly

LISA E JACKSON
Managing Director

Mr J Davidson
4 Avery Terr.
WORTHING BN26 4DA

Many business letters are nowadays addressed personally to individuals who are not known to the writer. Executives then prefer to reserve 'Yours sincerely' for letters to people they do know personally.

You must follow house style or the writer's preference at work, and copy the draft in the exam.

Check yourself

1 Did you spell the following words in full: House, Road, with, reference, secretary, responsible, with, Yours, Terrace.
2 Did you:

   a) remember to date the letter?
   b) use initial capitals as shown throughout the draft?
   c) use capitals for BIRMINGHAM, LISA E JACKSON and WORTHING?

C5 MARGINS

Read

In the exam you will not be penalised for your decision to use any size margin **unless** you leave less than 13 mm (½") at the top of the page, or as a left margin.

You will not be given any instruction to use a specific margin. You must make up your own mind.

You will be given A4 paper only (the size of the pages in this book) so there will be plenty of room for the material to fit on to the paper. A general rule for you to follow is to leave 25 mm (1") all round, that is:

- turn up at least seven lines from the top edge of the paper – this will leave six lines (25 mm) for your top margin;
- set a left margin of at least ten spaces from the edge of the paper (in **10-pitch**) or at least twelve spaces (in **12-pitch**).

It is better to turn up or tap along extra spaces just in case you miscount; it is not good practice to have margins that are too narrow.

If you are using word processing equipment your machine will work with pre-set margins and page lengths. You will be able to check that these are appropriate for use in the exam, that is, left and right margins **together** add up to at least 25 mm (1"). If you can, and wish to, reformat your page, you should follow the same guidelines on margins as for using typewriters.

LETTERS e, d, c

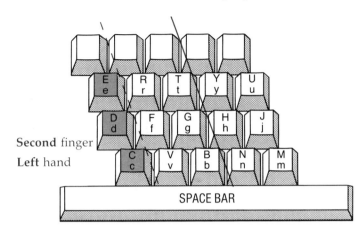

Second finger
Left hand

Get the *feel* of the three letters that you can type with this finger:

Type   d e c d e d c d e d c d

TWO FINGERS (left hand):

Type   freed fed cede   free breed reed tree greed

                deed ever verge   bed creed get greet edge

SHIFT key:

Type   Fred Edger

                                Dr G C Veter

TWO HANDS:

Type   the there three

                        berth Berty here jeered

                        hug hugged turfed hummed

                        turned gummed burned her centre

                        tender meter Brent juddered

BOTH SHIFT KEYS:

Type   Mr Greg Hute
            Rugby

            Dr Bert Unver
            Brent

            June Fentugh
            Bury

Note: Leave one line clear to separate different items.

C4 CAPITALS AND UNDERLINING (OR EMBOLDENING) FOR EMPHASIS

Type

BRIDGING LOANS

<u>Who Needs Them</u>?

You may need a bridging loan for house deposit if your ~~own~~ property is ~~soon~~ not sold by the time you need to proceed with purchase of your <u>next</u> house.

You may need a bridging loan for the TOTAL COST of your new one if Contracts are not signed on your present house in time for you to ~~pay for~~ complete the deal for the new house.

PROCEDURES

<u>Collateral</u>

You will have to satisfy whoever ~~agrees to~~ [grants you] the loan that the money will be paid back as soon as the sale of your ~~present~~ [PRESENT] house is completed.

<u>Interest</u>

Interest will ~~be~~ [depend] on the amount you have borrowed – probably on a <u>day-to-day</u> basis.

Check yourself

Did you:

a) use capitals for the two headings as shown?
b) use initial capitals and underlining, or embolden if your word processing equipment cannot underline, for the sub-headings as shown?
c) underline (or embolden) 'next' and 'day-to-day' as shown?
d) use initial capital for Contracts and capitals for TOTAL COST and PRESENT, as shown?
e) leave a clear line between headings and paragraphs?
f) leave an extra line space to show the start of the new paragraph in the first section if you typed in double-line spacing?

In the exam

In the exam you are expected to type words in capital letters, to type words with initial capitals, and to underline (or embolden if your equipment cannot underline) **as shown in the draft** (that is, the work you are given to copy).

FIGURES 3 TO 7 AND SYMBOLS

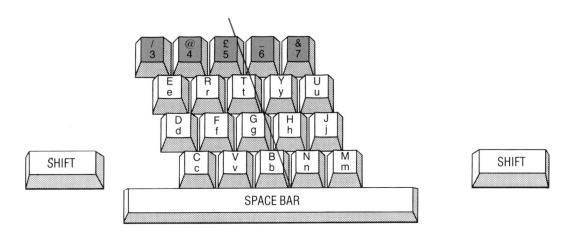

Reach up to the figures:

Type

de3 fr4 ft5 jy6 ju7

The 3 met Greg

Then 4 greeted Gert

6 hugged the edge but 5 deer turned here

37 The Hyde ˌHedgebury ˌRugby ˌCV37 6BM

36 red but 7 grey deer

Bert freed 367 by 6

Never defend the brute under the fence

Reference 37445 Term 4 Meter 6673 4 June

Leave 2 spaces to separate different items on the same line.

Use the shift keys over the figures:

Type

de3/ fr4@ ft5£ ju7& jy6_

Find out

If your keyboard has different characters on these keys from the ones shown here, you may wish to leave the following practice until you are using the fingers which type these characters on your keyboard.

Type

Church hymns 33/56/734/67

Ref 463/55

Fence Ref 6675 @ £56

Bench Ref 3637 @ £45

Three hundred grey deer fed <u>here</u>

The green jetty <u>deterred</u> them

Use shift lock to hold shift key down to underline long words.

Herbert & Jerry   37 Berry Rd   Bury

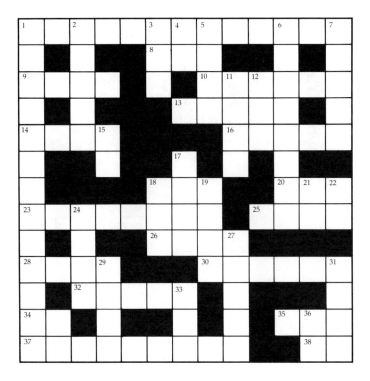

Clues

ACROSS

1 It tells and finds. (13)
8 Don't type on correcting fluid while it's this! (3)
9 Prevention is better than … (4)
10 Oil from them is used in cooking.(6)
13 Astronauts go out in this. (5)
14 Essential; has to be. (4)
16 A bald policeman? He appears on it. (5)
18 It cools you down. (3)
20 A gentle touch. (3)
23 Certain. (8)
25 Short note to a friend or colleague, used a lot in offices. (4)
26 Words. (4)
28 Related. (4)
30 BR vehicles. (6)
32 English for American elevators. (5)
34 Sounds as if comes after N. (2)
35 Yours and mine. (3)
37 Like 14 across: needs to be done. (9)
38 Afterthought in a letter. (2)

DOWN

1 We need this to live in. (13)
2 Words that state action in sentences. (5)
3 Between one and three. (3)
4 That is. (2)
5 We halt at a full one! (4)
6 Letters go inside it. (8)
7 Sugar and spice make food like this. (5)
11 After the deadline. (4)
12 Cold and slippy. (3)
15 Between one and three but shorter. (2)
17 What you must always put on a letter. (4)
18 If homework's not done, teacher will throw one! (3)
19 After this one. (4)
21 Before noon. (2)
22 Same as 15 down. (2)
24 Can't take any more. (4)
27 Yours … (5)
29 … Straits. (4)
31 Dear … (4)
33 Where the water is good. Leamington, for instance. (3)
36 Not down. (2)

For the completed crossword see page 88, **S**.

The letter 'e' is a **vowel** and is used to link other letters to make different word sounds.

Type edge edges merry ferry Henry benches munches
deed cede meet feet tree beer here
hugged tugged turned returned
grey
Herbert refer her Gert Bert germ fern terms

Think When you are checking your work, note the different sounds made by using the vowel 'e' in these words.

Read Nobody can help you with spelling unless you do this for yourself, that is note differences in words, their sounds and the way the sounds are made up by using vowels with other letters.

The keyboard exercises in this book have so far used the vowels 'a', 'u' and 'e'. 'Y' has also been used as a vowel. You may know which other letters are **vowels**. If not, look up the word 'vowel' in a dictionary; the five vowel letters should be included in the definition.

Aim to type the following in two minutes:

Type
```
        Fred Edger greeted them in Derby but then

        they judged the Rugby turf burned there
```

Check yourself Your work must be accurate, including capital letters as shown in the draft (what you are given to copy).

Type the following, starting new lines as shown:

Type Berty hugged June but even then
he jeered Greg
Henry hummed the tender tune
Betty jeered and juddered

RSA Core Text Processing Skills Figures 3 to 7 and symbols

In the exam

You may type in single- or double-line spacing without penalty, provided that you:

- type all paragraphs throughout a task in same line spacing;
- separate paragraphs by clear lines, and leave the same number of clear lines between paragraphs throughout a task.

Space between paragraphs in double-line spacing

In the typescript opposite it is quite clear where new paragraphs start, as the last line of each paragraph is short.

```
We shall not be able to follow

your directions without further

instructions.

On receipt of further and better

particulars we will proceed with

your order.

We look forward to receiving

your letter.
```

```
We shall not be able to

follow your directions

without further instructions.

On receipt of further and

better particulars we will

proceed with your order.

We look forward to receiving

your letter.
```

In this example there appears to be one paragraph only.

When typing in double-line spacing you must make it clear to the reader where paragraphs start and end.

The easiest and most generally used way to do this is to leave an **extra** line space clear between paragraphs in double-line spac-ing, e.g.

```
We shall not be able to

follow your directions

without further instructions.


On receipt of further and

better particulars we will

proceed with your order.


We look forward to receiving

your letter.
```

If you are using word processing equipment, insert an extra line ('return'), as well as giving your print instruction for double-line spacing.

When the typewriter line-space regulator is set at '2' you have to move the paper by means of the cylinder knob for a **single** extra line. The cylinder knobs (one at each side of the machine) usually turn up in half-line spaces so you may need to turn two 'notches'.

LETTERS w, s, x AND FIGURE 2

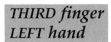

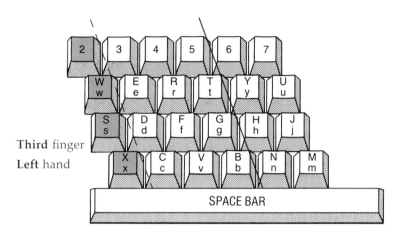

THIRD *finger* LEFT *hand*

Third finger
Left hand

SPACE BAR

Get the *feel* of the letters in the third finger:

Type

s w s w s w 2 w s x s x s

'W' helps to make many more words, e.g.:

Type

when we were went where whether

Names of people and places are **proper nouns** and *must* start with capital letters:

Type

Webb & Whyte	Webb & Whyte
Wunder Wyte	Wett Whuther
Wessex	Wessex

Names of ordinary things like mugs, jugs and rugs are **common nouns**, which do not need a capital letter unless starting a sentence.

'S' provides the **plurals** of **nouns** that you have previously typed, e.g:

Type

mugs jugs rugs grubs trugs tubs hymns thumbs gums

and some new nouns:

Type

shrub bush brush thresher setter dessert

You can now type addresses in full:

Type

Mr Greg Brunster	Dr June Fentry
22 The Hyde	27 Crumen Street
DERBY	RUGBY
DE23 7VB	CV26 2GN

Use your SHIFT LOCK to save time when typing whole words in capitals

---

SPACING AFTER A FULL STOP

If you wish to leave **extra** space(s) after full stops to show the ends of sentences, you may do so without penalty in RSA exams, provided you leave the same number of spaces after every full stop throughout a task. See also page 29 with reference to electronic typewriters and word processing equipment with automatic 'return' at the right margin.

Read

Line spacing

Single-line spacing means the machine turns up **one** line space on each 'return'; in double-line spacing the machine turns up **two** line spaces each time.

SPELLING PRACTICE 8

Practise using different line spacing in the following paragraphs.

a) Type in single-line spacing:

Type

> Matches will be played all thro' the first week in Apr. and will be open to all <u>novices</u>. Any employees at any of the factories or offices of the co. is eligible for entry provided he/she has not previously won a snooker tournament.

Check yourself

Did you type these words in full: through, April, company?

b) Type in double-line spacing:

Type

> Heats for the Winners' Contest will be held during weekends thro' May and June. Entry will be open to any employee of the co. who has won a snooker tournament within the last three years. This win may be in a co. contest, local sports or snooker club, regional tournament or national event. Entry forms are obtainable from Personnel Office, Sheffield Works.

Check yourself

Check your typing of the draft in b) with the following worked example:

```
Heats for the Winners' Contest will be held during weekends

through May and June. Entry will be open to any employee of

the company who has won a snooker tournament within the last

three years. This win may be in a company contest, local

sports or snooker club, regional tournament or national event.

Entry forms are obtainable from Personnel Office, Sheffield Works.
```

RSA Core Text Processing Skills   Understanding the syllabus: C3 Consistent style

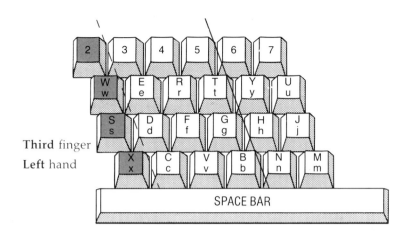

Third finger
Left hand

Use the letter 'x'.

Type   `exert Essex vexed Sussex next text texture`

Check   *Aim to type the following without stopping. Start new lines as shown:*
yourself

judges best better smut mutters
just text detest tested deters
dusted stewed west defends mends
where whether when went trusted

If you make errors in letters or spaces, type these four lines again.
(There is further practice using 'x' on page 40.)

Use 's' and 'es' to make **plurals** (words which mean 'more than one'):

Type   `shrub shrubs mug mugs tub tubs run runs hymn hymns grub grubs`

`bush bushes church churches dress dresses tress tresses`

*Type the **plurals** of the following:*

Type   `fender rung bug tube web thumb wrench bench mess`

Read and   Some of the words above end in sounds that can be spoken next to an 's'.
think   Others need a vowel sound between the end of the word and an 's'. Note
              for yourself which sounds need 'es'.

*Now type the **plurals** of the following words:*

Type   `reference fence dunce nudge defence`

Note for yourself the difference in sound when the above words were
made into **plurals** and **why** you added only an 's'.

Type

```
    116 Franchise Dr.◄
    CANTERBURY
    Kent   CT5 16TB


    Messrs J & G Berrows
    Sweetward St.◄
    INVERNESS   IV4 5GG

    Dear Sirs
                   to               last
    With ref./ your ⁄letter dated 19 of t̶h̶i̶s̶ month, I sh. be pleased to rec.
    a sample of your new product and to take part in your next survey.

    I enjoyed sampling your last product, wh. I have been able to recom. to
    several of my friends.
        application  has been returned
    The/form i̶s̶ ̶e̶n̶c̶l̶o̶s̶e̶d̶, duly completed and signed.  I have also completed
    the Section C of the (form) in which you ask each applicant to recom. at
    least one other reliable person to act as a researcher in your survey.

    Yrs. ffly.
```

Full stops show shortened words which must be typed in full. There are other examples in the paragraphs.

Check yourself

1 Did you spell in full the following: Drive, Street, reference, shall, receive, which, recommend, Yours faithfully?
2 Did you remember to date the letter?
3 Did you make all seven amendments?

Read

If you wish to use full punctuation in RSA exams you may do so without penalty, provided you remember to use the same style throughout a task.

Type

Copy the following, which will give you practice in typing punctuation:

```
Mary, who had been a teacher in her previous job, was working for a company in
Brentford.  Mary's work was divided between two sites: one at Brentford and
the other at Chingford.  Mary did not like working at Chingford.  The
supervisor knew this and one day asked Mary "Why don't you like Chingford?"
Mary was quite unable to give a reasonable reply; she had not thought out
her reasons.
```

Read

In the exam punctuation is considered part of a word. In the passage above, the apostrophes are in the words: Mary's, don't; opening quotation marks are part of: "Why; and all of the other punctuation marks are regarded as part of the word they follow.

If you leave out punctuation which is in the draft (or add punctuation which is not in the draft) you will be penalised for inaccuracy (word faults). You will also be penalised for inaccuracy if you do not leave space to separate words: a 'word' is regarded as including its following punctuation and space.

Count the word faults in the following by checking it against the paragraph above.

```
Mary,who had been a teacher in her previous job was working for a Company in
Brentford.  Marys work was divided between two sites; one at Brentford and
the other at Chingford.Mary did not like working at Chingford, The
supervisor knew this and one day asked Mary " Why don't you like
Chingford?"Mary was quite unable to give a reasonable reply: she had not
thought out her reason.
```

Check yourself

Check your list with the one given on page 88, **R**.

LETTERS q, a, z AND FIGURE 1

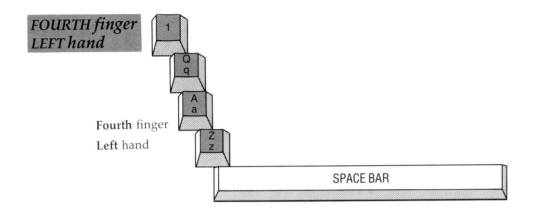

FOURTH *finger*
LEFT *hand*

Fourth finger
Left hand

SPACE BAR

The most important **letter** for this finger is the vowel 'a':

Type   a q a z a q a q 1 q a z a a a

Practice in using 'q' and 'z' is provided on page 42.

'a' links letters to make different vowel sounds:

Type   are rear wear as add afar agate

                    saw was swear dear fear afresh feared

Now you can type even more addresses:

Type   Mrs A W Asda
                          234 Great Avenue
                          ASHBY

You can also start a letter:

Type   Dear Aunty Ada   Dear Mrs Judger
            Dear Madam   Dear Ms Hearty
            Dear Mum   Dear Mr Wren
            Dear Dad   Dear Dr Tranter

You can also type more numbers, using the figure '1':

Type   12 West Street DEWSBURY HX11 2BE

            Rev J Smuthers 211 Arrun End   WASHBURN   DH12 12VX

C2 CLEAN WORK

Read

Part of your skill in text processing is your ability to handle paper without making it dirty or creased.

You can avoid 'dirty work' by:

- keeping your hands clean;
- keeping stationery in a drawer or flat in a folder;
- being interested enough to make a good job of text processing.

'Can't be bothered' is more likely to stop you succeeding than 'can't do it'.

KEYBOARD PRACTICE

1 Type the following, completing each word:

Type

```
Wh n you  re  mployed  s a typ st or word pr c ss r op r t r

you w ll b  pr c ss ng w rk f r others, who w ll b   nsulted  f

you th nk th  r w rk is of so l ttle  mport nce th t  t d es n t

m tter if it l  ks sh ddy.
```

Check yourself

Check your typing with the completed passage on page 88, **Q**.

2 Find the sentences from the word search on page 69.
Repeat typing these sentences for 2 minutes.
Aim to complete them twice without error.

Read

Creasing can happen when putting paper into a typewriter or a printer. Don't rush it. Make sure the bail (the bar with rubber rollers which holds the paper against the roller) does not stop, and crease, the top edge of the paper.

When using envelopes, use the paper release, and gently 'push' materials into position before taking off the paper release.

Creasing can also be caused by crumpling paper when picking it up – go **gently**!

C3 CONSISTENT STYLE

Read

Punctuation

The exercises in this book use **open style** punctuation. This means punctuation is used in sentences to convey meaning, but no commas and full stops are used in items that are not sentences, e.g. headings addresses, dates, after openings (e.g. Dear Sirs) and closings (e.g. Yours faithfully) in letters.

Type the following. Start new lines and leave lines clear as shown.

Type

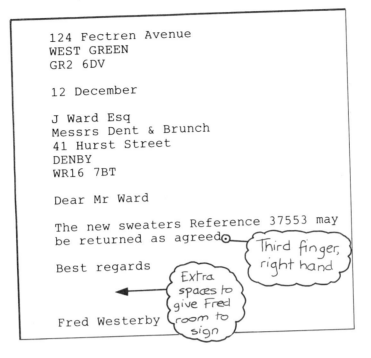

```
124 Fectren Avenue
WEST GREEN
GR2 6DV

12 December

J Ward Esq
Messrs Dent & Brunch
41 Hurst Street
DENBY
WR16 7BT

Dear Mr Ward

The new sweaters Reference 37553 may
be returned as agreed.

Best regards



Fred Westerby
```

Third finger, right hand

Extra spaces to give Fred room to sign

Address an envelope for the above letter. Use a size DL envelope (110 mm × 220 mm). For practice purposes you can fold A4 paper into three sections, each approximately the size of a DL envelope, i.e.

Type

Leave about 12 lines clear at the top (room for stamps, etc.)

Leave a left margin of about 65 mm (2½")

```
J Ward Esq
Messrs Dent & Brunch
41 Hurst Street
DENBY
WR16 7BT
```

Addressing envelopes on a micro-processor or word processor is difficult unless the machine is programmed to print at the right points. It is simpler and easier to use a typewriter for this task (see also pages 55-6).

In the exam

Read If you wish to use word processing equipment but your Centre does not have equipment that will take the stationery provided, you may use the stationery provided by your Centre. The person in charge of the exam (the Invigilator) will make a note on your answer book of the type of equipment you were using which meant that you had to use the stationery provided by the Centre.

If continuous stationery must be used, the pages must be separated before they are put into your answer folder (see syllabus items C1, page 9, and 4.7, page 10).

You may also transfer to a typewriter to produce the envelope. Alternatively, you may be provided by your Centre with labels for use with word processing equipment. An addressed label should then be stuck on the envelope provided by the RSA (see notes on pages 55 – 56 about good practice in positioning label(s)).

WORD SEARCH

Find and type the two sentences hidden in the following word search. Start at the top left corner. Words follow on down, up, across or diagonally, backwards or forwards. Each letter is used only once, but not all of the letters are used.

The first sentence starts 'Buy your own ...'

B	X	W	Y	P	Q	T	N
U	F	D	R	C	E	W	P
Y	Y	O	U	R	O	X	A
B	N	O	O	S	Z	Q	P
E	I	D	E	L	W	O	E
U	S	I	S	L	R	M	R
S	H	T	I	I	X	Q	A
I	T	T	S	W	P	Z	N
N	O	O	I	U	O	Y	D
G	B	O	D	E	A	R	T
X	W	E	T	S	A	W	O

Check your answer with the one on page 87, **P**.

LETTERS i, k, THE COMMA AND FIGURE 8

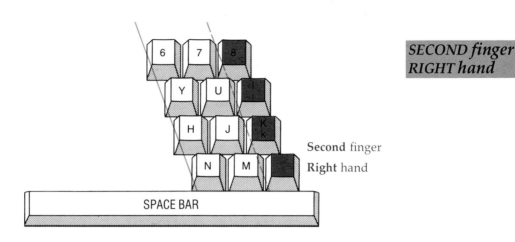

SECOND *finger* RIGHT *hand*

Second finger
Right hand

This finger gives you another **vowel**, 'i', as well as 'k' and the comma:

Type

```
k i , k i k , k i , k
```

```
kit kitten kitchens kitty skirt skate sketches skewer
```

```
skid skiff skimmed kick kid kiddy king knight knub kink kisses
```

```
sick stick trick Mick knitting kiwifruit kites
```

The **vowels** 'a' and 'i' go together to make the **vowel** sound in 'rain':

Type

```
rain drain grain train main maintain maintenance
```

Many words use the letters 'i' and 'n' joined together:

Type

```
in inn inwards infirm indeed intake drink ingrained income
```

```
bring string sink brink swing thinks stinks jinks
```

```
inject injury injuries injustice inside inhumane
```

Use *your* **shift** *key to type*:

Type

```
My key is where I said it was, Kitty
```

```
When I am near the stairs I can take my cake with me
```

```
Katy and I have three weeks at the ski run, and we can ski
```

Always use a capital letter for the word 'I'.

Type

```
he she they I we us me I them I he she I they I
```

Check yourself

Aim to type the following accurately and without stopping:

```
I did find the string where Katy said it was yesterday, Jacky
```

RSA Core Text Processing Skills Letters i, k, the comma and figure 8

C1 STATIONERY

Read

In the exam the answer-book provided for you to use will have in it:

- six sheets of A4 plain white paper (A4 is the size of the pages in this book);
- two DL manilla envelopes (see also page 55);

There will be two tasks to be typed on A4 paper, and the other task you have to complete is an envelope. You can see, there will be enough stationery for you to retype if you spoil your first attempt.

You must not use any stationery other than that provided by the RSA.

Type

FIRST-TIME ACCURACY

It is (oot) good practice to send out shoddy work rather than to use more stationery for re-typing. On the other hand, stationery is a large expense in most businesses, and those who waste it are not popular.

(Thee) is no. excuse these (day) for waste of paper. Modern (machine) give the operator time to make sure typing is accurate before it is printed. The extra time which ~~they~~ may be taken to get everything right is more than made up by the machines, which can type (or print) at very much faster speeds than a good operator.

SPEED COMES WITH PRACTICE

Some people wo[u]ld say you sh[o]uld practise speed from the beginning. This is true, but to put too much emphasis on speed at the expense of (accuragy) is to (forgdt) the advantages of new up-to-date machinery.

(One) of the reasons for the popularity of 'touch typing' was the increase in speed when time to keep looking at the machine (were) saved. Now it would be silly not to look at the machines which show you (wahat) you are typing, for the very reason that you should be able to correct it if necessary /before printing. Of course, it would be a terrible waste of time to have to look for ~~every~~ *each* key every time, so we do need to be able to use all fingers and to find each key from habit rather than have to wait till we can find it by sight.

Check yourself

Did you type the following words correctly: not, There, days, machines, would, should, beginning, accuracy, forget, One, was, what, before, each?

If you took longer than 45 minutes to type, check and correct this long passage (247 words), you need to speed up. In the exam you have to type 300 words in an hour.

Use the figure 8:

Type   81 Kinky Avenue   Kendy Edge   Keighsdean   Inverness   IV8 18N

            Ref 877/48

            38 Investiture Awards

            Credit 18 @ £82

            You can now type more dates:

Type   18 January and 28 February and 8 May and 18 June and 8 August

            8/8/88 and 8 March 88 and 18 January 87 and 8 August 88

            You can also type more openings and closings for letters:

Type Dear Madam/Dear Miss Birch/Dear Sirs   *shift character over the figure 3*

       Best Wishes/Sincere wishes/Best regards/Merry Christmas/New Year Greetings

            Practise using the comma:

Type   1, 2, 3 and 8 are the best

                        we may be here, there and everywhere

                        I want 8 knives and 8 saucers, Mary

                        the rug, the basin, the brush and the tray

Check   *Aim to type the following without stopping. (Repeat if you make errors.)*
yourself

                        There will be 8 girls here by 8 am

            Type these words without stopping:

                        ring bring fry draw try swing

            Now type these words again, adding 'ing' to each of them.

KEYBOARD PRACTICE

To build concentration, type the following, completing the words with gaps. The same letter completes all of the gaps.

Type

DECISION-MAKING IMPROVES YOUR TEXT PROCESSING PRODUCTION RATE

Product on work s equal n mportance to the learn ng of the keyboard
and bu ld ng speed and accuracy. However, students often learn to type
and are then expected to produce work w thout tra n ng n mak ng
dec s ons for product on typ ng and product on word process ng.

Product on not only nvolves sk lls n keyboard ng but also requ res
sk lls n mak ng mach ne adjustments, handl ng mater als, read ng
direct ons, plann ng the total job, proofread ng, correct ng errors
and d spos ng of the completed papers. Most of the t me-consum ng
elements of product on have noth ng to do w th speed of keyboard ng.

Check yourself

Check that you have typed 89 words (excluding the heading and including one hyphenated word). Then check your typing with the same passage given in full on page 87, **O**.

SPELLING PRACTICE 6

Type the following, spelling out all the shortened words. Remember, a full stop here shows that the word is shortened; it is not punctuation.

Type

CONTRACT ~~TYPING~~ PREPARATION

The final drafts ~~for~~ of the contracts must be recd. in Head Office by the first Wed. in Feb..

It is essential to rec. them by this day so that all Departments can check their content in time for completed ~~work~~ contracts to be recd. by the supplier before the end of Feb..

GOODS DESPATCH

Orders recd. ~~by~~ between Mon. and Wed. must ~~be~~ normally be despatched by Fri.. Orders recd. on Thurs. or Fri. must normally be despatched on Mon or Tues..

If goods are out of stock the customer must be sent an Order Acknowledgement form. This must include dates we expect to ~~be able to~~ rec. the goods from our works or suppliers.

Check yourself

1 Did you spell the following correctly: received, Wednesday, February, receive, Monday, Friday, Thursday, Tuesday?
2 Did you:

a) use capital letters exactly as shown in the draft?
b) include full stops to mark the end of sentences when *two* full stops were shown together in the draft?

RSA Core Text Processing Skills Understanding the syllabus: Reading for meaning

67

PRACTICE MATERIAL

1   Aim to type the following without error in one minute:

```
Tuesday, Wednesday, Thursday, Friday, Saturday, Sunday

Street, Avenue, Drive, Crescent, Terrace

Best wishes, Kind regards, Sincere wishes
```

2   **Use a dictionary**. Look up the word at the beginning of each line below and find as many words as you can which derive from (grow out of) the first word. Type these along the line. The first two lines have been started as an example for you. Aim for a total of at least thirty words overall.

```
busy business businesses

substitute substituted substitutes substituting substitution

secretary

advertise

define

receive

refer
```

Some suggestions are given on page 85, **A**.

3   a) Type the following:

```
26 Fendry Avenue
Kirby
WREXHAM   CH31 1BT

3 March

Miss J H Vanghi
71 Drench Avenue
CRANDEIGH HEATH
HR31 1EX

Dear Miss Vanghi

We have received a card advising that the curtains
are ready, but can they be fetched by Mr Jundah?

Best wishes
```

Find the ? key. It may be the same key as figure 8. You must use your shift key. If '?' is not there on your keyboard you should look to find it.

b) Type an envelope for this letter (to Miss Vanghi).
   Note: Users of word processing equipment may use a typewriter to produce the envelope in the RSA exam in Core Text Processing Skills (see also pages 55-6).

Type

116 Dragon St.
Petchley
LIVERPOOL L16 42BC

Mr J Parker
14 Haywood Cr.
DERBY DE15 8XG

Type an envelope, please

Dear Jim

I am sorry I have not had an opp. to write to you before, but I hope you will still be able to come to the meeting on Wed. of next week.

It will be a good opp. ~~for you~~ to refer to members those items wh. have been worrying us for some time. These opps. do not occur very often so we don't want to miss this one.

I look forward to seeing you.

Best regards

Check yourself

1 Did you spell these words in full: Street, Crescent, opportunity, Wednesday, which, opportunities?
2 Did you:

a) type today's date on the letter?
b) leave clear lines to separate the different parts of the letter?
c) type an envelope to Mr Parker?

WORD SEARCH

Find the following words in the word search. They may appear across, down or horizontally, forwards or backwards. Letters may be used more than once.

pitch	dictation	eg
type	address	draft
audio	date	underline
shorthand	RSA	

See page 87, **N** for the key to the word search.

H	Z	N	O	I	T	A	T	C	I	D
C	L	S	Y	X	P	I	C	T	H	A
T	Y	P	E	A	B	C	E	T	A	D
I	A	L	M	K	U	R	S	A	I	D
P	V	M	F	G	H	D	O	M	N	R
Y	O	D	R	A	F	T	I	E	G	E
C	X	D	N	A	H	T	R	O	H	S
U	E	N	I	L	R	E	D	N	U	S

LETTERS o, l, THE FULL STOP AND FIGURE 9

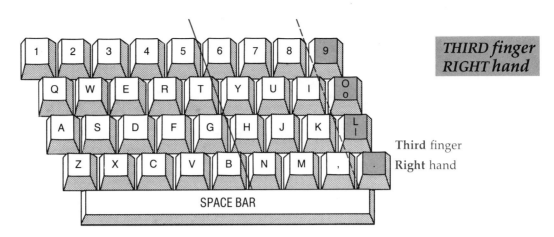

THIRD *finger* RIGHT *hand*

This finger gives you 'o', 'l', the full stop and figure 9. Get the *feel* of its keys into the finger:

Type

        l o l o l . l o l o 9 l

Use the figure 9:

Type

        29 Lolling Road

        2292 Lode Street

        99 lots of 9 loads

        1986, 1987, 1988

Now you can type more dates and all of the days:

Type

        9 May 1988, 19 June 1989, 29 July 1987, 9 August

        Monday, Tuesday, Wednesday, Thursday, Friday,

        Saturday, Sunday

Use the full stop:

Type

        I looked for a coat costing less than £29.95.
        Laura told us her holiday was lovely last year.
        Ling Loi received a letter. It was written in Chinese.

The capital letter at the beginning of a sentence is **essential** (it must be there).

Type

        I left my heart in San Francisco. This is an old song.

        The boat is in the harbour. Its flag is at half mast.

Reading for meaning

1

Retype the following, correcting words which are circled:

> It will (be) now have become apparent to you that we are (able) to come to your party tomorrow. We wish to apologise for this, but it was such short notice that we were unable to cancel several appointments already made. We do hope you have a good time, and (looked) forward to being able to attend your next event.

Check yourself

2

Read through what you have typed to check that it makes sense.

> I have today (hear) from the Solicitors (acted) for Mr Robinson to the (affect) that (there) client is (definite) interested in buying the property now offered in Leicester. He says that Mr (Robinsons) is (willeng) to pay the asking price. The offer is (make) on the understanding that the renovation work (are) carried out before the completion date.

Check yourself

3

Read through what you have typed to check that it makes sense.

> A Roof Overhaul (comprise) a complete service - all missing slates or tiles are replaced and all (lose) ones re-nailed; (guttering) cleaned all round; cracked cement (word) (repairing) and flashings re-proofed where necessary. (Not) extra charge is made for materials.

Check yourself

4

Read through what you have typed to check that it makes sense.

> Britons are (suppose) to be a nation of animal (lover) but all too often (family) take on pets without working out what the furry bundle is going to cost to keep. Neither a hamster nor a hound can exist on leftovers from the humans' table, and it does not (takes) long for most animals to eat their own purchase price in food. In (additon) there is the cost of sleeping accommodation, the vet's bills and kennel fees. A little (throught) in advance can avoid expensive mistakes.

Check yourself

Check the words that you have corrected against the lists on page 87, M.

The letter 'o' is another **vowel** which links letters to make more words.

Type   I will leave the locks on the letter shelf.

The show was lovely and very loud. It was televised for October.

We love the house at 99 Loveridge Road TROWBRIDGE.

Use your **shift lock** and **backspace** to **underline** on a typewriter.
Note: If you are using **word processing equipment** it may not be possible for you to print out with underlining (see page 17).

Type   <u>LESS</u> Trade Discount £9.99.

There are now <u>more</u> rather than <u>fewer</u> of those things.

Even if we <u>do</u> let you see our accounts, it is doubtful

if you will find out what you <u>want</u> to know.

His name is JAMES BARLOW and he lives at DERBY. He does <u>not</u>

know JERRY Barlow and <u>cannot</u> tell you where <u>he</u> lives.

Read   ## Spacing after a full stop

Some people like to separate sentences with **extra** space(s) after the full stop. This is good practice provided you learn to leave the **same** number of spaces **every time**. In RSA exams, you will not be penalised for the number of spaces you leave after the full stop *provided* that you leave the **same number every time**.

Note: **You need not** leave more than one space after a full stop. Many people prefer always to leave only one to avoid penalty when using a machine with automatic 'return' at the right-hand margin (e.g. electronic typewriter). This is because, once a right-hand margin has been set, this type of machine automatically turns up and returns to the left margin as soon as the space bar is tapped after a certain point on the line (this point is determined by where you set your right margin). If you tap the space bar more than once after this point (e.g. after a full stop), the extra space(s) will appear at the beginning of the new line; and this will be penalised in RSA exams.

Check yourself   *Aim to type the following without stopping*. Your work must be accurate in *every* respect, including capitals and underlining exactly as shown in the draft, that is, the original you are given to copy.

The losses <u>will</u> be refunded to the Company. Do not forget to check the Formal Accounts Statement prepared for issue on 9 October 1987.

KEYBOARDING PRACTICE

Type

To build your concentration, type the following, completing all of the words. You will soon see that the same letter fills all of the gaps.

```
We  re now  ble to  dvise you th t your order for G rden Tools is re dy
for desp tch.  However, we underst nd following your telephone c ll
yesterd y th t you m y prefer to collect these items.  We were un ble
to cont ct you by phone tod y.  The goods will be  v il ble for collection
on Mond y next,  ny time  fter 9  m.  However, if you do wish us to send
them, ple se let us know  s soon  s possible.
```

Check your work carefully. See page 86, **L** for completed passage.

SPELLING PRACTICE 4

Type

106 Penkridge Way
Threldon
HEATHWAY   OL41 2BC

Type an envelope

Dr J A Perkins
Greycourt
Denydown Rd.
FARNWORTH GU22 4DX

Dear Dr Perkins

Thank you for your letter received last Wed.. I note it will be necy. for me to obtain a health certificate and agree the best ~~thing~~ way is for me to attend the DHSS office next Thurs. afternoon.

I sh. be glad if you will make the necy. appointment, and I now return Form T1060 duly completed.

Thank you again for your attention.

Yrs. scly.

Check yourself

1 Did you spell these words in full: Road, Wednesday, necessary, Thursday, shall, Yours sincerely?
2 Did you remember to:

   a) type today's date on the letter?
   b) type an envelope addressed to Dr J A Perkins?
   c) type a full stop after 'Wednesday'?
   d) leave clear lines to separate each of the different items in the letter including the three paragraphs?

If you made error(s) try once more to produce an accurate letter. Remember, capital letters must be used as shown in the draft.

1   Type the following:

Eddy came here by cab. He then gave us an easy test and he even held an exam index card.

Dad ate at the cafe while the lady met Ted and Mum at the Cedar Halls.

The letter back to Mr Dexter started, Dear Charles, and ended, All the best.

(Leave a clear line to separate paragraphs)

Check yourself   Make sure that every word is accurate, including all capitals and punctuation.

2   Type the following note:

Tuesday

Dear Deanna

Charles must be at the Cheadle Vaults by 3 because he has a significant amount to do. I trust this will be arranged.

All the best.

Yours

(Leave a clear line to separate all of the different items.)

Check yourself   Make sure you have included clear line spaces to separate the different items in the note.

5

It is important to remember that we are always ..... busy
at Christmas and staff ...... cope with extra jobs during
this time. If you work here as temporary relief staff you
must .... on time so that we ... rely on your help. We
..... not employ you if you were not able to .... us an
assurance of punctual and regular attendance.

can   could   quite   come   cannot   give

6

We have 12 vacancies but only 10 applications. We shall,
........., be re-advertising the posts with a view to
attracting .... applicants. We do not anticipate being
able to appoint all of the 10 original applicants, ...,
so more than 2 new people will be needed.

however,   further,   therefore

7   Practise typing:

weather whether where were wear was went want when wearing

Then type the following, completing the gaps from the words above:

Very many men .... at the jetty .... the yacht ... checked
and searched. The rain ... heavy and the men .... wet but
they stayed because they .... heavy duty rain....
No women attended. We do not know ..... they waited, but ....
they returned the .... had improved. The rain had stopped
and the wind had dropped. We do not know .... or not any
illegal goods .... discovered on the yacht.

3 Type the following letter:

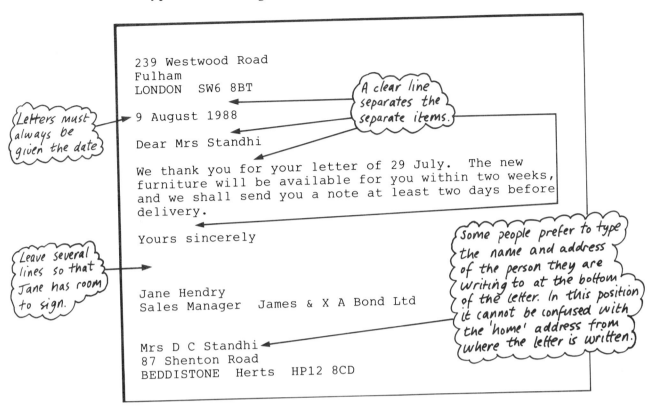

239 Westwood Road
Fulham
LONDON SW6 8BT

9 August 1988

Dear Mrs Standhi

We thank you for your letter of 29 July. The new
furniture will be available for you within two weeks,
and we shall send you a note at least two days before
delivery.

Yours sincerely

Jane Hendry
Sales Manager   James & X A Bond Ltd

Mrs D C Standhi
87 Shenton Road
BEDDISTONE Herts HP12 8CD

Letters must always be given the date

A clear line separates the separate items.

Leave several lines so that Jane has room to sign.

Some people prefer to type the name and address of the person they are writing to at the bottom of the letter. In this position it cannot be confused with the 'home' address from where the letter is written.

4 Type Mrs Standhi's reply to the above letter, including the envelope:

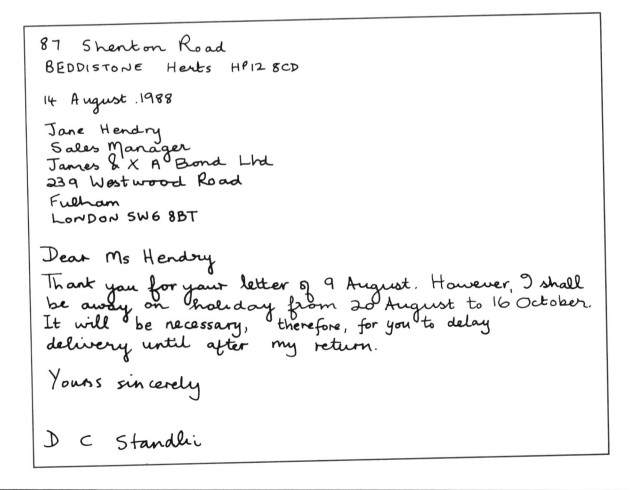

87 Shenton Road
BEDDISTONE Herts HP12 8CD

14 August 1988

Jane Hendry
Sales Manager
James & X A Bond Ltd
239 Westwood Road
Fulham
LONDON SW6 8BT

Dear Ms Hendry
Thank you for your letter of 9 August. However, I shall
be away on holiday from 20 August to 16 October.
It will be necessary, therefore, for you to delay
delivery until after my return.

Yours sincerely

D C Standhi

2

There are, .. course, many items .. stationery which are made .. paper, but stocks now include a great deal .. material for recorded dictation: tapes, discs, etc.

of

3

We thank you ... your letter dated yesterday .... which we note .... you will not be able .. attend the Business Conference in March. We shall .. pleased .. know whether or ... you are able .. be present at the Opening Ceremony of the Business Club .. 4 March. If not, perhaps you will .. good enough .. return the tickets .. that they may .. passed .. someone else.

to for be from on that be not so

4

Shall you be able to come .... us .... we go to the Exhibition in London next month? It ..... be helpful if you did come, so that you are there .... we decide .... to buy for the office.

with what when would

Read
Some word processing equipment can check your spelling. If you type incorrectly a word which is in the machine's dictionary some machines will automatically correct the word. Other machines will highlight the word on the screen to call your attention to it. You will then have to decide what the word should be and how to correct it. This is another reason to practise reading for meaning.

LETTER p AND FIGURE 0

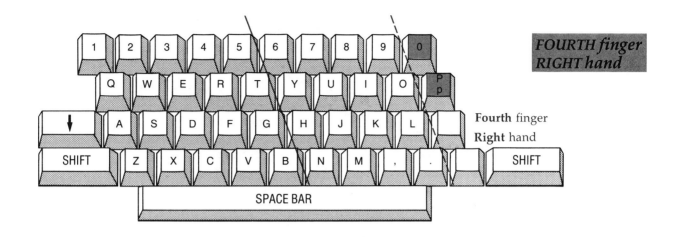

FOURTH *finger* RIGHT *hand*

Fourth finger
Right hand

This finger gives you 'p' and the figure '0':

Type

```
please plus pleat pleasure prayer price press

priority permit pence pests pounds point

possible apply application apologies apologise
```

You can now type all of the months:

Type

```
January February March April May June July

August September October November December
```

Practise the figure '0':

Type

```
10, 20, 30, 40, 50, 60, 70, 80, 90, 100.
```

You can now type all of the dates:

Type

```
10 April 1988

20 September 1989

30 April 1990
```

*Check
yourself*

Aim to type the following without any errors:

Please accept my apologies. My application
is dated 10 April, and I hope you will
grant me a priority permit.

Type the following correcting all of the circled words:

Type

> Animal (charities) (is) now taking greater steps to make sure that
>
> prospective owners know what they are taking on. They can (gives)
>
> guidance on what diet is needed, and what the cost of the foods
>
> (are) likely to be. A small dog may manage only 50p-worth of meat
>
> and vitamins a day, but a big dog such as a wolfhound may need
>
> about £3 a (daysspent) on (them). A dog does not live by food alone,
>
> and even if he is healthy and accident-free, there (are) still the
>
> cost of inoculations, and bills can quickly mount up if he becomes
>
> (il.1)

Check yourself

Did you type the following correctly:

charities (overtyping)   days spent (space needed)
are (related to 'charities')   him* (related to 'a big dog')
give (related to 'they')   is (related to the cost)
is (related to 'the cost')   ill. (keying error)

*could be 'her', but 'he' and 'him' are used throughout the article and, in any case, strictly-speaking, 'dog' is male.

Reading for meaning

- Shorthand-typists sometimes have difficulty reading a word in their shorthand.
- Audio-typists may not be able to hear a particular word.
- Handwriting may cause a typist or word processor operator to misread or to be unable to read a word.

All these are reasons why it is important to practise reading for meaning and filling the gaps.

Some of the exercises 'Reading for meaning' are more like games. Their purpose is to try to get you interested in words. Words are the **text** in **text processing**.

Type

Type the following, filling the gaps.

1

> There ... many occasions when it .. not possible to do just
>
> what you want to do, because it w.... cause inconvenience
>
> to others. In the future, there w... be other occasions when
>
> your preference ... be met. In the past there may have ....
>
> many occasions when others ...... their turn.

Check yourself

Did you include: are, is, would, will, can, been, waited?

THE SEMI-COLON AND THE COLON

Find out **Look at your keyboard.**

What does the little finger type on *your* middle row?

On most machines it is the semi-colon ';'.

Using the shift key, it types the colon':'.

The following practice material uses these characters. If your keyboard has these keys in a different place, use the finger you find most comfortable for them.

Use the semi-colon:

Type
```
The book was brought to Mike; it was bound in leather.

Sally was friends with Sashi and Bernica; so was her sister.
```

Use the colon:

Type
```
There are two colours: red and blue.

Our products are sold in the following towns: Leeds,

Harrow, Bournemouth and Brighton.
```

Check yourself *Type the following.* Remember, your work must be well presented as well as accurate. Always leave at least one extra space to separate sentences.

The prices are subject to VAT. There is also postage to be paid; the cost of packing is already included, but insurance premiums are:

£1.25 on orders up to £40;
£1.75 on orders over £40.

Always leave a clear line to separate listed items from the main paragraph.

COPYING PRACTICE

Aim to type the following without error. As the draft is in single-line spacing you may need to use a marker (e.g. a ruler or piece of paper across the draft, moved line by line) to help you to keep your place.

Type

```
I enclose a draft of the instructions for the Praestans Fleuriste.
Please check this through and make any alterations you feel
necessary. Although this looks fairly lengthy to me, it is within
the printer's limit and it should therefore be possible to print
it on the reverse of the cardboard packing lid. Instructions for
other species will follow in a day or two.
```

Check yourself

1 If you made any error in words, make one further attempt to type accurately.
2 Did you use capital letters as shown in the draft?
3 Did you leave the same space each time after full stops?

B6 CORRECTING ERRORS IN THE DRAFT

Read

```
The survey (have) been quite encouraging for the last (eightleen) months
```

The following exercises are intended to help you to see relationships between words. In the example above, the word 'have' is related to 'survey'. The word 'survey' is singular (only one survey) so it should be followed by 'has' instead of 'have'. It is obvious that in the word 'eighteen' the typist or word processor operator has made a keying error.

Type the following, correcting all of the circled words:

Type

```
The capital of the (Uited) States of America is (washington). Many

people say "New York" when asked to name the USA's capital.

Perhaps this is because NY is the largest city. London is both

the capital and the largest city in the (Uited) Kingdom, but the

size of the city (do) not determine whether or not it should be

the capital. The seat of the (cojntry's) Government, the place

where Government offices and departments (is) situated and where

Parliament meets is always designated capital of the country.
```

Check yourself

Did you type the following correctly:

United
Washington
does (a singular verb) related to the subject 'size' (a singular noun)
country's
are (related to 'offices and departments' which is a plural subject)?

KEYBOARD CONSOLIDATION

You have now practised typing with all eight fingers, all the letters of the alphabet and punctuation marks as well as figures.

You now need to concentrate on developing your **copying** skills as well as practising regularly to keep up your accuracy.

Use your machine manual

The following exercise is in double-line spacing, that is, leaving alternate lines clear. Your machine will automatically type in double-line spacing providing you adjust it accordingly. **Check in the index of your machine guide** under the heading 'line spacing' or 'line-space regulator'.

Type

```
Television commercials screened during news and current

affairs programmes are more likely to be watched than

those shown in light entertainment programmes, according

to a new survey. The research shows that viewers not

watching advertisements are most likely to be switching

channels, reading, or making themselves a drink, and

almost a third of the TV audiences can be lost to advertisers

in such ways.
```

Check yourself

Remember, do not just read your typing. Follow the draft (above) with your finger, and follow your typing with your other hand.

Did you use capitals as shown in the draft? When you are instructed to copy a draft, you should do so in every respect.

But: if your machine types in a different **pitch** (size of typeface) from the machine used for the draft it may not be sensible to use the same line endings shown, and you should use reasonable margins for your machine.

Note: It is not good practice to leave less than 13 mm (½") margins. If you file your papers in a loose-leaf binder (sometimes called a 'ring file') you will know that holes might be punched through typing that is too close to the left-hand edge of the paper.

Check the typing below from the handwritten draft. List any errors you find. You need to be extra careful when checking unfamiliar words.

Typed	Handwritten	(Line Number)
PROTOASCO-	PROTOASCO-	1
MYCETIDAE	MYCETIDAE	2
Eurotiales	Eurotiales	3
Microascales	Microascales	4
Onygenales	Onygenales	5
Laboulbeniales	Laboulbeniales	6
ASCHOHYMENO-	AsH ASCOHYMENO-	7
MYCETIDAE	MYCETIDAE	8
Erysiphales	Erysiphales	9
Pezizles	Bu Pezizales	10
Tuberrales	Tuberales	11
Helotiales	Helotiales	12
Phacidailes	Phacidiales	13
Xylarriales	Xylariales	14
Hyppocreales	Hypocreales	15
HETEROBASIDIO-	HETEROBASIDIO-	16
MYCETIDAE	MYCETIDAE	17
Protoclavariales	Protoclavariales	18
Auricularialas	Auriculariales	19
Tremellaels	Tremellales	20
URedinales	Uredinales	21
HOLOBASIDIO-	HOLOBASIDIO-	22
MYCETIDEA	MYCETIDAE	23
Aphyllophorales	Aphyllophorales	24
polypoales	Polyporales	25
Boletailes	Boletales	26
Agaricales	Agaricales	27
Ruspulales	Russulales	28

Check yourself   Check your list with the one given on page 86, **K**.

Retype exactly the handwritten list in the exercise above. Note that each separate list has a heading in capitals. Clear lines separate lists from headings.

Check yourself   You will *really* need to follow the draft and your typing letter-by-letter to be sure of this one!

THE DASH/HYPHEN KEY

Read

This key is not in the same position on every QWERTY keyboard. You need to look and find where it is on your particular machine.

Type

```
Hyphenated words are regarded as one word in RSA exams,

eg pre-eminent, co-operation, pine-covered, Miss Smith-Denvers,

sub-standard, shorthand-typist, audio-typist, line-by-line.
```

Check yourself

A hyphen is part of its word. Make sure you do not leave any space within a word (including either side of a hyphen) or your work will be penalised in RSA exams.

Type

```
We do not - nor do we intend to - have any large trees in our

garden. The fruit trees - apple, pear, cherry - are all shrub

or dwarf varieties which will not grow higher than 3 metres.

Notice was given to you - in our letter dated 29 November last -

that these were to be planted and offering you the chance - which

you did not take - to object.
```

Check yourself

The dash is a punctuation mark. The accepted way to type it is to include a space between it and each word. Make sure you never confuse the dash with a hyphen: always leave a space before and after it.

Reading for meaning

Type the following:

The office hours are 9-12.30 with a mid-morning coffee break 11-11.15; and 1.30-5 with a mid-afternoon tea break 3-3.15.

The firm is forward-looking, using up-to-date methods and machinery. Their activities - which are many and varied - include operation of cross-channel ferries.

Check yourself

In the exercise you have just typed there are two dashes only, in the final sentence. The words with hyphens are: mid-morning, mid-afternoon, forward-looking, up-to-date, cross-channel.

Note: When the dash key is used for the word 'to', it does not matter whether you include spaces or not:

e.g. 11–11.15 *or* 11 – 11.15.

But you must type every example in the **same way every time**.

The way you choose to type particular items for which there are no rules is your **own style**. **Good** style includes typing the same sort of item in the same way every time.

PRACTICE MATERIAL

'Paying meticulous attention to detail' means making sure that **every little thing** is exactly right.

Make a list of the lines where there are differences between these two columns:

	Column 1	Column 2
Line 1	21334	21134
2	A-/-32B	A-/-23B
3	Fellowes	Fellowes
4	Order	Order
5	Price	Prices
6	K-881;2	K-881_2
7	Fen2ill*do"brixiff	Fen2ill*do'brixiff
8	111	1111
9	1002	102
10	buggleygum	bugglygum
11	Mrs Anthea Feachindrow	Mrs Andrea Feachindrow
12	Mrs Alicia Frenchiston	Mrs Alice Frenchistone
13	Statistical	Statistical
14	ETA:1200hrs	ETA:1200 hrs
15	MOD, POBOS 127B, RG21 2BR	MoD, POBOX 127B, RG21 2BR
16	SLAPONS, WAEC, WP, CTQ	SLAPONS, WAEC, WP, CTQ

Check yourself Check your list with the one on page 86, **I**.

Make a list of any errors in the typed working of the handwritten draft below:

Young cyclists need to learn how to behave on the roads. Bicycles must be in good condition. Checks are needed before longer journeys are undertaken in the holidays. Children who are not old enough to ride bicycles should be encouraged to play in areas put aside for their own use or in their own gardens. Play equipment should not be defective. Fish ponds and water butts could be covered with protective netting. Broken glass must be disposed of, and garden machines and tools put away when not in use. Chemicals, such as weed-killers, should be locked away and never transferred to an unlabelled container.

```
Young cyclists need to learn how to behave on the road. Bicycles
must be in good condition. Checks are needed before longer journeys
are unddertaken in the holiday. Children who are old enough to ride
ride bicycles should be encouraged to play in areas put aside for
their own use or in their own gardens. Play equipment should not be
defective. Fishponds and water butts could by covered. Broken glass
must be disposed of, and garden machines and tools put away when
not in use. Chemicals, such as weed killers, should be be locked
away and never transferred to unlabel
```

Check yourself Check your list with the one on page 86,**J**.

RSA Core Text Processing Skills Understanding the syllabus: B5 Unfamiliar and/or foreign words

QUOTATION MARKS AND THE APOSTROPHE

Read   These keys are not in the same position on every QWERTY keyboard.
            You need to look to find them. On many machines the double quotation
            mark " is a shift character over the figure 2, and the single quotation or
            apostrophe key ' is often the shift character over the figure 8.

Type

```
She said, "We shan't be going to the Saturday show".

"Why not?" asked Brian.                          Typist: Please
                                                 copy exactly

"Because we have already booked to go to London by coach."

Brian replied, "Oh, I had forgotten that".
```

Check   Did you type the quotation marks and full stops in exactly the order in
yourself which they appeared in the draft?

Type

```
"The title of the show is 'Pennyfarthing Sounds' and we are

hoping there will be at least a fairly large audience."

"Well, I hope you do well and all enjoy yourselves. I'm quite

sorry I won't be there."

"Pat will be particularly sorry. She thought you knew the

date and mentioned your name yesterday as one of the people

who wanted tickets."

"She must have forgotten the trip to London. I'll ring her."
```

Check   Drafts in the RSA Core Text Processing Skills exam will *not* include
yourself   deliberate errors in the use of quotation marks and apostrophes for you
             to correct. You should always copy the draft.

Type

```
The boys' college was two miles from the girls' school, and the

girls did not know the way. The boys did not believe them and

thought the girls just didn't want to go to the disco. The mother

of one of the girls offered to drive them to the college, but

she would be leaving at 9 o'clock.
```

It is not always possible to tell where apostrophes should be placed by
reading for meaning. It is therefore particularly important to copy
accurately.

B5 UNFAMILIAR AND/OR FOREIGN WORDS

Read

Material in books and in exams must be fictional, that is, made up. So as to be as realistic as possible, real town names are used, but streets, districts and postcodes may be imaginary.

If you live in a town which is used in a draft, you may know that some of the details are not real. You must not let this 'inside information' lead you to change the draft. Leave it alone!

The principle is that you must copy names and addresses exactly. Customers and other people may be offended if you do not take the trouble to get their names right; and if you make mistakes in addresses you may cause delay.

If you think a mistake has been made in real life, you can double-check by asking or looking up records. In the exam you cannot do this and must rely on what is given to you.

Concentrate on accurate copying so that you will be in the habit of taking great care with names and addresses when you are at work in an office.

Type

381 Kording Road
Traydingley Heath
PETERBOROUGH PE47 8SS

Mrs June Keller
Hand House
Brotherington
OXFORD OX27 2AA

(Type an envelope)

Dear Mrs Keller

I have used PRAXITELES products for 20 years and have never had cause for complaint. However, the Praxiprod Garden Hoe is not strong enough to cope with the work as advertised. The Ativeadros Hoe is far superior. I hope this information is useful to your survey.

Yours faithfully

Check yourself

Did you:

a) date the letter?
b) separate the different parts of the letter with clear space?
c) type an envelope to Mrs Keller?
d) use capital letters and initial capitals as shown in the draft, i.e. PRAXITELES, Praxiprod Garden Hoe, Ativeadros Hoe?

Read   Verbs make statements in sentences, saying what the subject **is** or what the subject **does**, e.g. in the sentence, 'The cat sits on the mat.'
–'The cat' is the subject;
–'sits' is the verb, telling what the cat **does**;
–'on the mat' is the description, that is, it completes the sentence by telling us more about the statement.

Type the following two exercises:

Type and read

```
A "sentence" with only a subject, that is a noun, does not
qualify as a full sentence, eg The cat ...

A "sentence" with only a subject and a description is not a
sentence either:  The cat on the mat ...

'The cat sat on the mat' includes the verb, and is a proper
sentence.
```

The red table
The red table is
The red table is in that room.

We
We thank
We thank you for your letter received yesterday.

I
I do not
I do not know how old you are.

She
She will go
She will go to Bournemouth on 10 December.

Always leave at least one line without any typing on it, to separate different items and paragraphs

---

Read

If you use a microprocessor or word processor that is not specially programmed to print on to envelopes, you may move to a typewriter to type the envelope.

Alternatively, your exam centre may provide you with label(s) for use with your word processing equipment. This label, when addressed by you, should be stuck on an envelope so that it could be used to send the letter in the normal way.

This will be equally acceptable to the Examiner provided that the label is accurate. It is not good practice to stick the label right at the top of an envelope or too near the left edge (see page 55).

Type the following letter, together with an envelope:

Type

> 79 Hallett Road
> Trentham Common
> SWINDON   SN18 12TG
>
>
> Mr J R Singh
> 42 Barrows Lane
> HUDDERSFIELD   HD27 8QQ
>
> Dear Mr Singh
>
> Thank you for your letter. Unfortunately, you failed to include the completed form, although your letter refers to it.
>
> If you will forward the form to us we will process your requests as soon as possible.
>
> Yrs. ffly.
>
> James Pollock

Check yourself

Did you:

a) date the letter?
b) leave a clear line to separate different parts of the letter, i.e. address, date, name and address, opening, paragraphs and closing?
c) leave several clear lines for Mr Pollock to sign?
d) type an envelope to Mr Singh?

BRACKETS

Read

The brackets are usually on the same keys as the figures 8 and 9, and you have to use the shift key for them. They are not in the same place on all QWERTY keyboards.

Check where they are on your keyboard.

Type

```
The new Manager (she moved here from Hereford) started work on

1 January 1987. Her office needed redecorating (it was previously

a store-room) so the Manager shared the office of the Sales

Manager (Export) until the end of February. The new Manager's

secretary joined the company in March, at which time a word

processor was installed (linked to the existing computer system)

for his exclusive use.
```

Check yourself

You should leave *no* space between the bracket and the word to which it is attached.

Type

> The elements of cost of telephone calls are (a) time of day when the call is made, (b) distance, (c) length of time the call takes. Telephone costs can be controlled by various means but most important (and perhaps most difficult) is the restriction of employees' personal calls.

Check yourself

You should have checked the exercise you have just typed against the draft above. Now look at the worked example below to make sure that you have typed it correctly.

```
The elements of cost of telephone calls are (a) time of day
when the call is made, (b) distance, (c) length of time the
call takes. Telephone costs can be controlled by various means
but most important (and perhaps most difficult) is the restriction
of employees' personal calls.
```

Remember, when using brackets and apostrophes, spacing and placing must be accurate.

B4 ENVELOPES

DL size = 110 mm × 220 mm   Manilla = brown paper

It is a good idea to leave room for stamps and Post Office cancelling marks (about 12 lines at the top)

It is good practice to leave a good left margin (about 65 mm – 2½") so that the address is approximately in the middle of the envelope

Mr and Mrs Fletcher

23 Woodridge Avenue

Witton

BIRMINGHAM   B6 8TD

Read

In the RSA exam in Core Text Processing Skills you will be supplied with two DL manilla envelopes.

You will be asked to address only one envelope. The other is for you to make a second attempt in case you spoil the first one.

Type envelopes for the following two letters:

Type

116 Falkiss Road
~~CORB~~ COLCHESTER
CO16 2TD

Miss J Patel
27 Heath Way
READING   RG22 1XD

Dear Miss Patel

I am ii r

for

Cottage Three
Hall Row
STOCKPORT   SK16 12B0

Mr J O'Donovan
4 Twelfth Street
SOUTHALL   UB40 6OK

Dear Sir

Th

Unless you are given special instructions to the contrary, the envelope must always be for the name and address to which the letter is being sent.

KEYBOARDING: BUILDING STAMINA

Read

It is better to stop and take a short rest after typing, say, each paragraph, than to become bored and tired. Accuracy is far more important than speed now that machines are so fast. Many electronic typewriters can 'save' a line until you get it right, and word processors do not print until you 'tell' them to do so. The machines can then print your corrected work very quickly indeed.

Type the following, aiming to complete it within 45 minutes:

Type

RECORDS, TAPES, COMPACT DISCS

We all know that big business results from the millions of records, tapes and compact discs sold in this country, Europe, USA and now Russia and China. Most of us think of music as the material recorded, but there is also a large sale of plays, readings of books and poetry, and lectures on a variety of media. In other words, people apparently like listening to the spoken word as well as the whole spectrum of musical expression.

It is the pop-music world which advertises heavily and is constantly referred to in television and radio programmes as well as the press and magazines. However, by far the largest audience for records, tapes and compact discs (mostly albums) is that for classical music. No one artist is as spectacularly successful, perhaps, as some of the pop idols. Nevertheless, some of the pop stars come and go, whereas many of the classical stars have been selling recordings for between twenty and thirty years. No one recording may have sold a million copies, but over all the recordings and years such individuals can claim to have sold many more copies than some of the more talked-of pop star performers.

If you have not noticed them before, you will be surprised how many recordings there are in the shops which are not of music but of words: Shakespeare's plays, books - both classical and popular literature - and poetry. In addition, there are dozens of recordings accompanied by books for children.

```
7 Elizabeth Road
Parkfields
WAKEFIELD West Yorkshire
WF11 88BT
```

Type an envelope to
Mrs J Benton
14 Mary Lane
BRADFORD BD62 14DX

```
Dear Aunty Joan

Thank you for your letter.  I shall def. come to Jill's birthday
                                                           on
party on Sat. week but I am not sure if I sh. come to stay/Fri. night.
                                          she cannot be def. about the
My Mum may be going to see Gran on that Fri. and will not be back in
          she will be backhome.
time to take me to the station.  Mum is going to ring Gran on Mon. to
                                                                  the
check, their plans and I will send you a card on Tues. giving you
def. time and day when I sh. come arrive.

Love
```

Check yourself

1 Did you spell the following correctly: definitely, Saturday, shall, Friday, definite, Monday, Tuesday?
2 Did you remember to type:

   a) the date?
   b) the full stop after 'home'?
   c) the envelope?

Read

It is not usual to include the name and address of the person that the letter is being sent to in a very informal letter such as this. The 'home' address is still put at the top so that the person reading it can immediately see where it is from.

WORD SEARCH

Find the following words written in full in the word search:

rec.	co.	sh.
sep.	refs	w.
sec.	bel.	recom.
bus.	wh.	

Words may appear across, down, upwards, diagonally, and forwards or backwards.

Letters may be used more than once. (A key to the word search is given on page 86, **H**.)

S	B	E	L	I	E	V	E	Y	S
B	E	M	H	C	I	H	W	R	E
U	W	P	H	Y	T	R	S	A	C
S	D	I	A	B	A	F	M	T	N
I	A	E	T	R	N	R	S	E	E
N	C	G	J	H	A	P	U	R	R
E	L	L	A	H	S	T	V	C	E
S	R	E	C	E	I	V	E	E	F
S	C	O	M	P	A	N	Y	S	E
D	N	E	M	M	O	C	E	R	R

EXTRA PRACTICE: s, x, w

Type

s x s w s x s w s x s w 2 w s x 2 x s

ex extra exclude excluding exclusive exit exile

Read   In the following passage, 'ex' means 'out of' or 'from'.

Type

The price of this car is £6,397 ex works. This means the cost

of delivery from works to the garage will be extra.

The car may be supplied ex stock. This means there will be no delay

because the vehicle will be taken out of the stock of cars waiting

to be sold.

The price is exclusive of tax, which is an extra 15%.

Look at your keyboard to find this special sign for 'per cent'. You usually need to use the shift key with it.

Check yourself   First, concentrate on the figures and punctuation. Secondly, read each word to check your accuracy. Thirdly, read again to make sure you have not omitted anything.

Did you show clearly where new paragraphs start, e.g. by leaving an extra line space clear between paragraphs in double-line spacing?

Aim to type the following without error within 2 minutes:

Type

wax waxed waxing waxes text texture textile example exemplary

exact exactitude excitement exercise extent examinations

Check yourself   Did you spell every word accurately? Errors are often made in: exemplary, exercise, excitement. Make sure you don't risk exam penalties through careless copying of accurate drafts.

Read

You may have typed the last exercise either in single- or in double-line spacing. When you are given no instruction it is sensible to use the same line spacing as in the draft.

It is important that the reader can tell when a new paragraph starts so you should always leave a clear line to separate paragraphs. One clear line is already there in double-line spacing, so it is general practice to leave at least two lines clear to separate paragraphs in double-line spacing.

On a typewriter, to leave *one* extra line when the line-space regulator is set at '2' you have to move the paper manually (turn the 'cylinder knob' – there is one at each side of the machine).

If using a microprocessor or word processor, you will need to insert an extra 'return' ready for when you set your machine to print in double-line spacing (see also page 34).

SPELLING PRACTICE 2

Type

30 Pebble Mill Drive
CANNOCK
Staffs WV30 16TX

~~STAR~~
Stralls Agency Ltd
Fachy Industrial Park
HEDNESFORD Staffs
WV 36 10BA

Use double-line spacing and type an envelope

Dear Sirs

We bel. you have recently started bus. as a Text Processing Agency. Please let us/have full details of services provided by your co., as we bel. we may be able to do bus. together. Our co. has recently increased its bus. in text processing and we may be able to sub-contract work at peak times. In this way it may be possible for our two cos. to develop a ~~good~~ profitable bus. relationship.

We look forward to hearing from you.

Yrs. ffly.

Check yourself

1 Did you spell the following correctly: believe, business, company, companies, Yours faithfully?
2 Did you:

    a) remember to type the date?
    b) type an envelope to Stralls Agency Ltd?
    c) use double-line spacing and leave an extra space to mark the new paragraph 'We look forward ...'?
    d) remember the comma after 'company' (third line in the letter)?

EXTRA PRACTICE: LINE SPACING

Aim to type the following without error in 5 minutes:

Read and type

> The verb in the sentence is essential so that we know what the subject is doing, has done, or will do.
>
> For example, it is no use saying 'Your letter' and stopping. It makes no statement about the letter.

Check yourself

If you used double-line spacing, did you show clearly the ending of the first paragraph and the beginning of the second, for example, with an extra space?

Remember, typing includes checking and correcting your work. In 5 minutes, your work must be accurate in every respect.

Type and read

> In the exam you must copy the punctuation in drafts (the work you are given to copy).
>
> When copying handwriting it is sometimes easy to mistake a comma for a full stop or the other way round. Because they are next to each other on many keyboards it is also easy to miskey full stops for commas, and vice versa.
>
> If you read and follow the meaning of what you type it is likely that you will avoid errors in copying punctuation.

> Cats are generally cheaper to keep. A pony, ~~really~~ which is the dream of many girls, is perhaps the most expensive. Most children have to be satisfied with hamsters or gerbils. The running costs of budgerigars are not high, although a good bird might cost ~~ten pounds~~ £10 or so to buy in the first place, and of course it will need a cage.
>
> Tropical fish are cheap to buy, but remember the heating and the plants. They need a tank and some equipment to clean the bottom of it. A sad feature of this budget is the need to replace fish quite often, because the death rate is so high.
>
> to oxygenate the water.

Check
yourself

- First, check your copying letter-by-letter.
- Secondly, read through your work for meaning (you may have misread a word when you typed it, and again when you checked it with the draft).

Note: Amendments are simple to cope with. Yet many candidates make mistakes in exams when following them. In particular, punctuation marks (such as the full stop in the balloon above) are forgotten.

B3 SPELLING

Read

Even typists, word processor operators, shorthand-typists and audio-typists are not expected to know every word, its spelling and its meaning.

If you work in an office dealing with technical matters, you will soon become familiar with a variety of specialist terms, but you will receive plenty of help with them at first.

When processing text your real responsibility is to **check**. It is easy to pick out technical or difficult words to look up – but if you have to look up every word that has more than one syllable you will never have time to finish your work! So you must have a bank of words that you can be sure about.

As a start, you need to know and understand the words that are listed in the syllabus of the RSA Core Text Processing Skills exam (see pages 7 – 8). In the following pages, you will find these words included in spelling practices 1 to 10. They are also used in other exercises throughout the practice material.

SPELLING PRACTICE 1

Type the following, completing the shortened words throughout. Remember that several of the full stops used here show the words which are shortened. The full stops should not be typed as punctuation.

Type

```
ADVERTS. FOR ACCOM.

Please note all adverts. must be registered with the office before being
placed on this Notice Board.  This includes all requests for accom. as
well as advertising of accom. which is vacant.

Please also note the office cannot deal with enquiries for accom. except
in official hours.  All adverts. must be paid for at normal weekly rates.
```

Check
yourself

Check your work carefully. Did you spell *advertisements* and *accommodation* correctly?

EXTRA PRACTICE: q AND z

Type   a q a z a q l q a q a z a z a q z q z a q z a

maze amazed amazing mazes size outsize sizes zoo crazy puzzle

puzzled quiz quizzed squeezing quartz quart quarter queried

Read   'Q' is never used in English words without being joined to 'u'.

Type   When they arrived, there was a queue to get into the discotheque.

Consequently, they did not get in until quite late.

Their tickets did not qualify for a discount. Jacqueline and David

paid a price equal to the cost of Dave and Jan's tickets. Jacqui

subsequently requested a refund and the management did not quarrel

with this demand.

Check yourself   Concentrate on the words with 'qu', first. Errors often occur in: Jacqueline, discotheque.
      Did you leave the same number of spaces after each full stop?

Aim to type the following without error within 2 minutes:

Type   qualified quay quiet quilt quote quest queer quarry quality

squire squeal squirrel squall equity earthquake requirement

Check yourself   If you made any errors, make one further attempt. If you still cannot achieve the above aim, make a note to try again later.

B2 AMENDMENTS

Read   Text processing includes working from drafts which contain amendments, that is, crossing out and instructions to change or add text.

So long as you concentrate, and follow the meaning of the passage, this should give you no trouble at all.

However, typists and word processor operators do incur penalties in exams by not making amendments accurately.

Practice material in this book includes amendments that will be used in drafts for the RSA Core Text Processing Skills exam:

- change, e.g.

> We do not believe you paid the bill.
> I refer to your letter dated 29 September
> (the company / received today.)

- leave out, e.g.

> please do not ~~not~~ hesitate
> ... there will be ~~be~~ more than is required ...

- add, e.g.

> How often do
> Do you use your phone?
> Do you think we shall be able to use the phone?

or balloon with arrow, e.g.

> You may have a separate business phone. Or do you rely on your home telephone for business purposes? (sometimes have to)
>
> Wall telephones can be very useful, particularly in kitchens or industrial room is at a premium. (Surroundings where)

Type the following, making all of the amendments (that is, changes) shown:

Type
> The research confirms many of the accepted views: that breaks in the middle of programmes hold the attention of viewers better than ~~the~~ breaks between programmes; that men are more likely to stay in front of the set; and that breaks in the peak periods are watched by more (than women) of the audience than those in the early evening.

RSA Core Text Processing Skills   Understanding the syllabus: B2 Amendments

51

EXTRA PRACTICE: THE FULL STOP

Read   Sentences are made up of **nouns** (subjects), **verbs** (statements about what the subject **is** or **does**) and **descriptions**. They can appear in any order. For example,

Your letter [*the subject*] requesting delivery of the goods on your order [*description*] arrived [*verb*] yesterday.

Type

We
We shall be
We shall be glad of your co-operation in this matter.

By next Thursday
By next Thursday we
By next Thursday we shall have
By next Thursday we shall have the goods.

With reference to your letter of yesterday,
With reference to your letter of yesterday, we
With reference to your letter of yesterday, we have passed
With reference to your letter of yesterday, we have passed
your request to our Accounts Department.

You need to **check** your understanding of the parts which must be included in a sentence. This will help you to read for meaning, which will improve your copying and checking skills. Decide which of the above words or phrases act as: *description*; *subject* (who or what the sentence is about); *verb* (saying what action the subject takes, has taken, or will take). Then look at the answer on page 85,**B**.

EXTRA PRACTICE: p, r AND y

Type   pray prayer practice praying prays pretty preferred

prepared apply applying applied application ample amplify

amplification amplified dimple print professional public prism

Read   Practice is a **noun**.

'The doctor's practice is in the High Street.'
'Practice helps you to learn to type fluently.'

Type the following reply, and an envelope:

Type

24 Hastings Road
TWICKENHAM TW13 9PP

Ms Mary Dessingham
Wyndham Gorge
HARROGATE   North Yorkshire
HG12 7DD

Dear Ms Dessingham
Thank you very much for your letter.
I would like to visit to see your Aunt's diaries and
have tried to ring but have not managed to get a reply.

I am going on holiday next month and am visiting Scotland.
As I shall be travelling by road it occurred to me that
I could stop in Harrogate on the way home. Would
Thursday 29 suit you?

Perhaps you would drop me a line before then. If
your letter arrives after I leave for Scotland, a
message will be sent to me.

Yours sincerely

Jane Klitcher

Check
yourself

Did you:

a) date the letter?
b) leave at least one clear line space between paragraphs and separate
    all of the other different items (e.g. addresses, date, opening)?
c) leave several lines clear to give Jane room to sign the letter?
d) type an envelope to Ms Dessingham?

Use your dictionary	*Look up 'noun' and find its meaning, to help you to type and complete the following exercise.*

Type

```
A noun is a w... used as a n... for a thing, place or person.

Names of particular p..... or p....s must be given a capital

letter. Names of businesses, associations, societies and clubs

must also have c...... l.....s and you should always use a

capital letter for the word 'I'.
```

Check yourself

Make sure the above paragraph, with the words you have used to complete it, makes sense. (To help you to check that you have filled in the gaps with the correct words, this paragraph has been completed for you on page 85, **C**.) Then check for any keying errors. You should have the same number of spaces (at least one) after each kind of punctuation mark.

Aim to type the following, without error, in 3 minutes:

Type

```
spray sprint sprinkle spring sprightly play plant plait please

plinth pleasure plug pound pond pork pointing position positive

pod up upper
```

Read

'Typing' does not just mean keying. Within 3 minutes you should be able to:

- key-in the exercise;
- check your work;
- correct your work as necessary to provide an accurate copy of the exercise.

Read for meaning and type

Put full stops in the following passage, to make proper sentences and good sense:

```
With reference to your letter dated 10 January I believe you

will be able to move into your new home next month Mr Jones

has already paid a deposit on the house in Poole and expects

to move no later than 15 March Contracts cannot be exchanged

until Building Society approval is given
```

Check yourself

You should have typed three sentences. (See page 85, **D** for paragraph with full stops inserted).

B1 DATES

Read

Every letter must show the date on which it is typed. It is part of the job of text processing to know this and you should remember to include the date on each and every letter you type without having to be told each time.

Type

```
Wyndham Gorge
HARROGATE   North Yorkshire
HG12 7DD
```

```
Miss J S Klitcher
24 Hastings Road
TWICKENHAM   TW13 9PP

Dear Miss Klitcher

Thank you for your letter received yesterday. It is true that
I have my Aunt's diaries here. They were left by my Grandfather,
Kevin Lutens, who had been given them for safekeeping when my
Aunt left for Canada. You will understand that they are precious
to me and that I would not want to part with them.

If you wish to visit to inspect the diaries you would be welcome.
I am in most days but would prefer you to phone beforehand to
arrange a visit. My number is Harrogate 8253191.

I look forward to meeting you.

Yours sincerely



Mary Dessingham
```

Check yourself

- Did you remember to type today's date on the letter?
- Did you type an envelope to Miss Klitcher?

Style

Read

There is no need to worry about the style you use for the date. The most common style is: day, month, year, e.g. 22 September 1988.

If you prefer to use another style, you will not be penalised in RSA exams. The most important points are:

- remember to date letters;
- use the right date;
- type the date accurately.

In the following passage each sentence has at least one word with some letters missing. *Type the paragraph, completing the words by reading the whole sentence(s) for meaning.*

The book shelves were very untidy with about fifty books on each shelf. Sandra and Jason were asked to tidy them and to sort the books into alphabetical order. Sandra thought they should use the names of the authors to do this but Jason wanted to sort the titles into alphabetical order. After arguing for several minutes they went to the office to ask Alphonse to explain. He was speaking on the telephone and they had to wait a few more minutes. By then it was nearly lunchtime so after Alphonse had explained that the authors should be in alphabetical order and that he would help, they all agreed to start the sorting in the afternoon.

Check yourself Check your typing carefully; then turn to page 85, **E** to find the completed paragraph.

Type *Add full stops, and type the following:*

With regard to your request for a discount our Branch Manager informs me that the prices quoted already include a reduction of 10% I hope you will agree this makes the cost of the Garden Tools very competitive Invoice No 627 is enclosed for goods supplied in August and we hope to receive your cheque soon

Check yourself You should have typed three sentences. (See page 85, **F** for paragraph with full stops inserted).

Read The above exercises were to give you practice in reading for meaning, which helps you to read handwriting and to find errors in your own work.
In the RSA Core Text Processing Skills exam some handwritten words will be shortened for you to spell in full (see list on pages 7 – 8). Some typewritten words will be circled for you to correct errors. You will *not* have to fill in gaps of any sort.

EXTRA PRACTICE:
using eight fingers

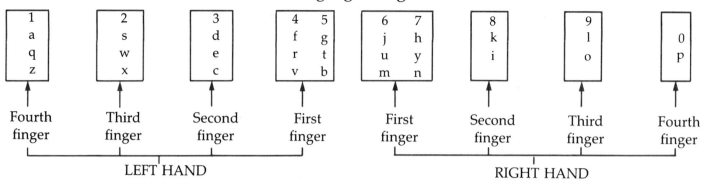

Type   a b c d e f g h i j k l m n o p q r s t u v w x y z

1 2 3 4 5 6 7 8 9 0 0 9 8 7 6 5 4 3 2 1

1a 2s 3d 4f 5g 6h 7j 8k 9l 0

a;sldkfjghfjdksla; a;sldkfjghfjdksla; a;sldkfjghfjdksla;

These make useful warm-up drills each morning or at the beginning of each practice session.

Aim to complete the following passage accurately within 10 minutes:

Type   I do not know how old I was when I first began to have a deep love for the sea and all that is in it. I began by reading all the sea stories I could lay my hands on, and have even written some myself from my own experiences, which have been both many and varied.

As I look at that last sentence I feel that it is quite amazing how important this love of the sea and all things to do with the sea has become to me.

Check yourself   After working for 10 minutes your work should be accurate in every respect. Each full stop should be followed by the same number of spaces, and paragraphs should be separated by at least one clear line space.

EXTRA PRACTICE:
using the first and second fingers of the left hand and first finger of the right hand

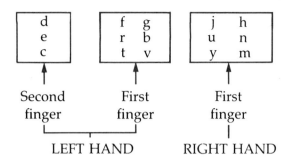

Type   mug jug hug hen ten men

Make up and type more three-letter words using only the letters typed by the two first fingers of the left hand and the first finger of the right hand.

Type   verb curb numb curt germ

Make up and type four-letter words using the letters typed by the same three fingers as above.

Type   nerve curve verve under dunce trend crude thumb

To your list add five-letter words still using only the letters at the top of this page.

Type   better fender gender recede hunter mender nugget

Now add words with six letters from the same range of keys.

Try to get at least twenty words in each set of three-, four-, five- and six-letter words. You can include names of people and places.

Type   tethered deterred crunched referred reference hundred

Add any words that you can find with seven or more letters from the same keys.

Check yourself   Check your list with the words suggested on page 85, **G**.

Aim to type the following in 1 minute without error:

Type   Mr Hugh Denby entered the church but then he met Gerry Hunter

_____
RSA Core Text Processing Skills   Extra practice: first and second fingers of the left hand/first finger of the right hand

46

EXTRA PRACTICE:
using the first, second and third fingers of both hands

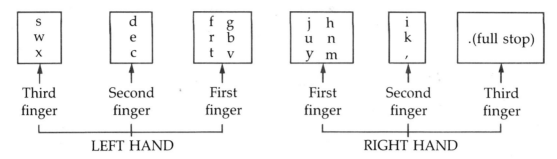

Type   sweet singers greet the merry men in the swinging sixties

Check yourself   If you make error(s) retype once, typing as quickly as you can, and a second time slowly to make sure you make no mistakes.

Aim to type the following accurately in 2 minutes:

Type   In the summer Cedric, residing in The Cedars in West Cheshire,

invited his friend, Herbert Kent, with his wife, Betty.

Check yourself   Your work must be read, typed, checked and, if necessary, corrected in the time allowed.

Aim to type the following accurately in 2 minutes:

Type   They went in their new vehicle, but were very undecided where the best scenery might be seen during the tide.

Check yourself   Make sure you include all punctuation exactly as in the draft.

Aim to type the following accurately in 2 minutes:

Type   We were there when they decided ~~them~~ the new, higher kitchen ceiling needed brightening. They used fresh designs with lighter tints. This succeeded in giving better, ~~lighter~~ brighter light.

Check yourself   The above exercise, compared with the previous one that you had to type in 2 minutes, has more words and is amended. If you can complete this, without error, in 2 minutes, you are making good progress towards the exam.